the Groacher file

A Satirical Exposé of Detours to Faith

by Kenneth L. Gibble

San Diego, California

LuraMedia™

to my daughter Katie,
who loves a good story
and who is still teaching us
why Love is what the story is all about

LuraMedia
7060 Miramar Road
San Diego, CA 92121

Library of Congress Cataloging-in-Publication Data

Gibble, Kenneth L., 1941–   *1-89*
   The Groacher file.

   1. Christianity—20th century. 2. Christian life—1960–
3. Satire, American. I. Title.
BR125.G46 1988   248.4   88-13479
ISBN 0-931055-55-5

Quotation from THE PRESENCE OF THE KINGDOM by Jacques Ellul,
© copyright 1967, The Seabury Press, New York, used by permission.

Quotation from MONSIGNOR QUIXOTE by Graham Greene, © copyright
1982 by Graham Greene. Reprinted by permission of Simon & Schuster, Inc.,
New York.

Quotation from LIGHTEN OUR DARKNESS by Douglas John Hall,
© copyright 1976, Westminster Press, Philadelphia, used by permission.

The Scripture quotations, unless otherwise indicated, are from THE
REVISED STANDARD VERSION OF THE BIBLE, © copyright 1946, 1952,
1971 by the Division of Christian Education of the National Council of the
Churches of Christ in the U.S.A. Used by permission.

PUBLISHER'S NOTE

*This book is a work of fiction. Names, characters, places, and incidents either are
the product of the author's imagination or are used fictitiously.*

And oftentimes, to win us to our harm,
The instruments of darkness tell us truths,
Win us with honest trifles, to betray's
In deepest consequence.

— *William Shakespeare*
MACBETH

Contents

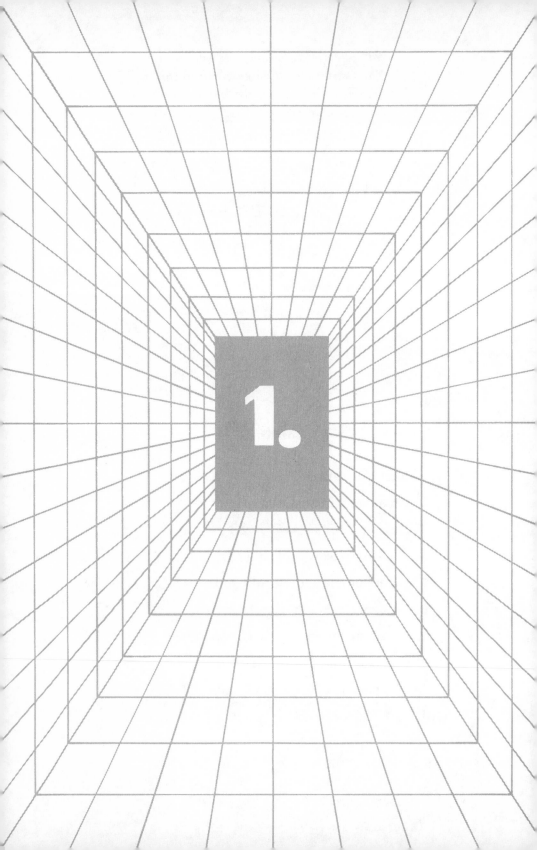

First Encounter

Had it not been for my ignorance of computer technology, Groacher's exploits would doubtless have remained unknown to me. Even now, I am not permitted to divulge the details of how I am kept informed of Groacher's doings. But I can tell you how my first encounter came about.

It was while enmeshed in a late night session of frustration at my computer that I first stumbled across the evidence of Groacher's existence. As a bewildered newcomer to the personal home computer scene, I had just spent the previous five hours fighting my way through a bewildering maze of cables, disks, instruction manuals, and countless other computer technicalities. Now bleary-eyed and irritable, I stared in disbelief at what I saw in front of me. The screen on my monitor read:

To: Raphael of Dawn
        The Court of Celestial Light
        Heaven

From: Pharnum Groacher
        Agent for Subversion and Corruption
        Grovedale Division

My first reaction, not surprisingly, was to suspect that someone was perpetrating a practical joke. I also vaguely recalled reading about "computer viruses" and wondered if something bizarre had been planted into my new software. Little did I realize that this was the first of many documents to become known to me, documents which would all bear a name that was to become intimately familiar in the months ahead: Pharnum Groacher.

Throughout my reading (and frequent re-readings) of these subsequent documents, my suspicions of their genuineness remained. How I finally had my suspicions laid to rest is neither an appropriate topic for discussion here nor of particular interest to readers. Suffice it to say that I did, in time, receive verification of both Groacher's existence and his demonic activities.

You see, Pharnum Groacher is a devil. That is, he is an agent for none other than the Prince of Darkness. . .or, as he is called at various times, Satan, Lucifer, Beelzebub, Old Scratch.

Sometimes I have wondered, "Why me?" Why did these documents show up on my screen? At other times I have wondered what to do with the documents. Should I go public with them? Would people believe their existence? How would people respond?

My reasons for finally deciding to make the Groacher documents available to the public are not, I confess, purely altruistic. While I do hope the papers will throw some light upon the methods employed by demonic agents, and thus prove a warning to people of all walks of life, I have a less honorable motive as well. Simply put, I hope to atone for some of my writings of which I am not particularly proud.

Under a well-disguised pseudonym, I have published stories and books which, while they have provided a healthy boost to my personal income, have not been of sufficient artistic or moral caliber for me to take pride in. In other words, I have sold out. It may be that publishing the correspondence in the Groacher file will strike some as a tawdry effort to "even the score" in whatever moral balance sheet we are finally to be judged. However, I cannot worry about the opinions of others. It is enough for me that the mere anticipation of going public with the Groacher correspondence has eased my conscience sufficiently to end an insomnia that has plagued me for the past several years.

Contents of what I have called "The Groacher File" are published here with virtually no editorial changes except for occasional corrections in spelling and grammar. Any editorial comments appear in italics. For the convenience of the reader, I have sorted the correspondence into chronological sequence and grouped the memos according to subject.

Make of them what you will, but at least now I will not be the sole bearer of the information contained in The Groacher File.

2.

Groacher's First Assignment

Documentation relating to Pharnum Groacher's first field assignment is scanty. The only written record available is the correspondence which follows. The first letter, written by Groacher himself, reveals that he has been assigned to the Grovedale Church, an apparently thriving congregation in the United States. The specific location of the church is not made clear, but an educated guess would place it in a mildly affluent suburb of a major metropolitan area.

Early in this letter Groacher gives the impression that he is a demonic agent with extensive field experience. He states that Grovedale is a "new assignment" which is his reward for "a lengthy period of diligent and imaginative work."

This statement reveals one of the great difficulties in a study of the Groacher file contents. Like all demonic agents, Groacher is skilled in the lie. But not greatly skilled . . . he is actually a rather obvious liar, though he does sharpen his skills in time. Other of his colleagues, and especially his superiors, are far more adept at twisting the truth than Groacher. Nevertheless, one must read everything Groacher writes with full awareness that he will mislead, exaggerate, and prevaricate whenever he thinks it suits his purpose. His claim to be an experienced agent is a good example. Later documents in the file prove conclusively that the Grovedale Church is actually his first assignment after graduating from the Brimstone Training School. Thus a healthy skepticism about anything Groacher writes is advised.

It should also be noted that no record exists of the original memo, to which Groacher is apparently replying.

To: Raphael of Dawn
        The Court of Celestial Light
        Heaven

From: Pharnum Groacher
        Agent for Subversion and Corruption
        Grovedale Division

Re: Your proposed offer

Distinguished Adversary:

I confess to no little surprise at receiving your memo yesterday. Had anyone suggested to me that personal exchange between your world and mine were possible at all (except, of course, at the highest official levels), I would have laughed in his face.

I confess also to considerable surprise at the contents of your missive. Behind all your heavenly jargon — 'The Divine Prerogatives,'' ''Blissful Design,'' ''Providential Prudence,'' etc., etc. — I detected the unmistakable invitation to negotiate or, as the earthling Americans are fond of saying, to make a ''deal.''

Your letter *did* satisfy my curiosity on one point, and in fact, confirmed my suspicions. I had always wondered, and thought it quite likely, that your system of organization had progressed much as ours had. I'm sure you'll agree that the old system of assigning an agent (angelic, in your case; diabolic, in our case) to work with individual mortals has outlived its usefulness. It may have served well enough in simpler times; but, as our teachers at training school insisted, new realities demand new methods. The sociological approach makes so much more sense, don't you think? With one agent assigned to a business office, another to a country club, another to a school, still another to a local political party, we can each specialize according to our training and personal preference. We have the advantage, too, of conferring with our colleagues on the progress or, more happily, the regress of the poor creatures who come under our jurisdiction.

In fact, just two days ago in one of our conferences, we hit upon a strategy we have great hopes for. Naturally, the details are classified, but I can tell you that it involves a bank, a group of politicians, and (I'm proud to say) the church to which I've been assigned. This kind of collaboration makes possible the achievement of a delightful level of mistrust, injustice, and the inevitable resulting despair which our old methods could never have achieved.

One thing I'm not clear on, however, is whether or not an assignment to a church represents a desirable or undesirable position for you heavenly agents. (By the way, I know you prefer the term ''angels,'' but I'm so used to our term that I find it hard to make the switch.) Looking at it from your point of view, I suppose being made the spiritual overseer of a group of Christians could be a real honor. The possibilities for the advancement of your cause are greater than if you were placed in charge of a labor union, let's say, or the Chamber of Commerce. On the other hand, it could be that your superiors regard looking after a church as requiring less effort and creative ability than would a secular group. To be blunt, maybe you are a church angel because you can't cut it out there in the real world.

The truth is, I have no way of knowing if you are a top-notch agent or a mediocre one. I don't mind telling you, however, that our philosophy in Hell calls for assigning only the best agents to church groups. Our reasoning is that, while Christians do have

unlimited potential for doing the will of the Lord of
Heaven, they have an equally unlimited potential for
doing the will of the Prince of Darkness. With proper
cultivation and encouragement, our agents can convert
simple goodness into smug self-righteousness; sincere
devotion into a marvelous, lip-smacking fanaticism.
Need I remind you that some of the earthlings' most
vicious and bloody doings have arisen from their
religion?

You can see, therefore, that my new assignment
to the Grovedale Church is a step up for me. It represents a reward for a lengthy period of my diligent and
imaginative work on behalf of our Malevolent Lord.

But now to the business at hand. In your communiqué you state that the good people of Grovedale
have been under your care for the past ten years and
that you have been pleased with their progress. You are
much too modest, worthy counterpart! Our intelligence
network reports that this church represents a real
danger to our Cause: its members are united in their
commitment, and they are reaching out to others in
Christian love, to name just two of their repulsive
accomplishments. I congratulate you on your
achievement.

What prompted your letter to me, I am sure, was
the headway I have already made in the Grovedale
ranks in the few short months I've been there. I am
overjoyed that I've so quickly been able to throw the
proverbial wrench into your plans by dropping a few
half-truths here and there. My predecessor at Grovedale,
as you probably know, was incompetent. Hers was a
political appointment; she is, in fact, the niece of
Grubgruel, the District Supervisor.

At any rate, your offer, as I understand it, is that
you will allow me to have full ownership of five

Grovedale members, whom you describe as "influential and respected believers." In return for these five souls, I must agree to ask for reassignment to another post.

Your proposal has its attractions, I admit. It would be a feather in my cap to announce the capture of five mortals in so short a time. But I do not intend to accept your offer. First, I obviously have given you a scare or you wouldn't have even made the offer. I intend to pursue my advantage. In fact, with hard work and a little luck, I just may be able to win over a dozen or more key lay members — and maybe even the pastor — before the year is out. I've noticed that the Reverend Mr. Bliss vacillates between feeling positive and negative about his work. If I can catch him in one of his low periods. . .well, the Devil only knows what might happen.

Secondly, I'm not fooled by your self-styled, "generous" offer. The five persons you are so willing to sacrifice are, in no particular order of unrighteousness, 1) a gossip; 2) a hypocrite; 3) a constant complainer about everything; 4) a marginal member who usually makes it to church only on Christmas and Easter; and 5) an ungenerous soul who has plenty of money to spend on his personal hobbies of oyster fishing and coin collecting, but who screams bloody murder when asked to make a financial commitment to the church.

Admit it: you'd be relieved to get rid of the pack of them. So it's "no deal," my celestial rival.

Yours,

Pharnum Groacher
Agent for Subversion and Corruption
Grovedale Division

P.S.   How can you heavenly creatures continue to delude yourselves? Ultimate victory belongs to the Forces of Darkness. Look what we've got on our side at present: the ever-growing spread of nuclear weapons, a burgeoning international debt, and *Penthouse* magazine. You haven't got a chance.

The following document is obviously a reply to Groacher's memo.

To: Pharnum Groacher, Agent
         Grovedale Division
         Nether Region
         Hades

From: Raphael of Dawn
         The Court of Celestial Light
         Heaven

Re: Your transfer

Sir:

I found your recent letter interesting...and amusing. Despite your glowing version of what you regard as your devilish accomplishments, the truth is that you are in deep trouble. I happen to know, for instance, that your financial records have been under close scrutiny by the Infernal Revenue Service. It seems you've been abusing your expense account privileges. Naughty, naughty! You, of all creatures, should know you've got to give the devil his due.

Then there's the matter of your being "promoted" to the Grovedale assignment. Horsefeathers! This is your first chance to put into practice what you learned in training school. If you fail in this assignment, well...as you would so appropriately put it...where you'll end up, the devil only knows.

And, of course, your inference that I was offering you five souls as a bribe to get rid of you is too ridiculous for comment. My suggestion that you pull out of the Grovedale assignment voluntarily was for your own good. Better to ask for a transfer than to get kicked out. Face it, Groacher, you are in over your head. By getting out now, you may save your skin — at least for the time being. You are way behind on your quota, and soon there will be the devil to pay. (My apologies for these witticisms, dear Groacher; bad jokes are the one temptation I've never been able to overcome.)

Actually, I've grown almost fond of you, watching you from this distance. You try so hard, in your own bumbling way, that I almost find myself pulling for you sometimes. It's rather like rooting for Charlie Brown...you know, the cartoon character...to win a ball game. You are sure he never will win, but just once you hope he'll get lucky. I can almost hear you muttering to yourself, wondering as Charlie Brown does, how you can lose when you're so sincere.

And really, Groacher, that postscript you wrote — you remember, about nuclear weapons and *Penthouse* magazine? Can you possibly be so naive? Whatever are they teaching these days in your training schools? Surely you must know that, in the long run, such things are more useful to our side than to yours. An experience of evil, while it causes much regrettable suffering, brings mortals to an awareness that, without the Almighty, they are destined to perish. Or, to quote a book I know you are thoroughly familiar with (and choose to cite frequently for your own purposes), "the wages of sin is death."

No. The things you really have going for you are of a much different kind. The people of Grovedale are more likely to be turned aside from the paths of right- eousness by a rising stock market, by the power of positive thinking, by life insurance, or by a pizza "with everything." Not that any of those things is evil in itself. They are, in fact, desirable; the more of them people have, the better people feel. Until finally, they begin to believe life can be truly fulfilling to the degree they possess these things.

Besides, how can you possibly put *Penthouse*, a magazine intended mostly for folks who enjoy feeling "naughty" about sex, on the same level with nuclear war? Maybe that's why you'll never be able to make it in the big-time temptation business, Groacher. You have no sense of subtlety. In a word, no *class*.

My advice to you is to take what you can get out of the present situation and request a transfer to a less demanding post.

Cordially,

Raphael of Dawn

Judging from the urgency of the document which follows, it is safe to assume that Groacher's reply was almost immediate. (None of the documents in the Groacher file is dated).

To: Raphael of Dawn
         The Court of Celestial Light
         Heaven

From: Pharnum Groacher

Re: New terms

Sir:

   For reasons which I am not permitted to
divulge, I am willing to come to a gentleman's agreement regarding the Grovedale situation. However, in
addition to the five persons we have already discussed,
I am also demanding custody of the Collins couple,
new and potentially dynamic members of the church,
as well as John Stern, long-time member. The sacrifice
of these three, while it will represent a setback from
your point of view, will nonetheless be a small price to
pay for ridding yourself of my influence. I promise to
see to it that my successor to the Grovedale project will
be an easy-going, unambitious demon.
   With this success under my belt, I hope to be
able to get at least a junior level appointment to an
influential organization — like the World Council of
Churches or maybe even the Vatican. Let me know
immediately if you agree to my terms.

           Sincerely,

           Pharnum Groacher

That Groacher's first field assignment came to an inglorious end is confirmed by the following document.

Summons
Perdition Intelligence Agency
Doomsgrave Square
Hades

To: Agent Pharnum Groacher

From: Superintendent Morosely Clamper, PIA

Re: Misdemeanor charges

You are hereby summoned to report to the Belial Office Building, Perdition Intelligence Agency, Room 666. You will do so without delay. You will answer charges against you of misuse of expense monies, of willingness to conspire with the Adversary for personal gain, and of general incompetence.

Emphatically,

Superintendent Morosely Clamper

P.S.   Dear Pharnum, haven't seen you since you graduated. Sorry to have to send you this, old boy, but rules are rules. Guess you hadn't heard I'd moved up over here at the PIA. We've had you under surveillance for some time now. It's routine for us to give close attention to new field agents. Never thought you'd fall for that phony communiqué-from-Heaven business. It's one of our oldest techniques, and we thought maybe by now word had gotten around about it. But really, Pharnum, you should have known that the Other Side doesn't make deals of any kind. We got you with the goods, I'm afraid. Cheer up, though. I'll do my best to get you off easy. After a decade or so of collecting sin statistics for the Hades Census Bureau, maybe I can even land you a modest post again — say in one of the wilderness galaxies, or, if you want another assignment on Earth, how about Tibet? After all, what are fiends (oops), I mean *friends* for?

Regards,

Morosely

Groacher In Vermont

Ensuing reports in the Groacher file reveal that not only was Groacher found guilty of the offenses he was charged with, he was also reduced in rank, removed from his post at the large and influential Grovedale Church, and demoted to a new field assignment: a small farming village in upper Vermont. It is from this post that Groacher filed several reports, among them the following.

To: Ferule Flogmaster
          Regional Director of Agents on Probation
          Stygian Creek Drive
          Hades

From: Pharnum Groacher

Re: Third quarterly report

Dear Director:

      This is my third report since my assignment to the town of Needmore, Vermont. As you know from my first two reports, it took me only a very short time to assess the situation, to determine who the influential people were, and to come up with some ideas for doing the most damage possible in the name of our Malevolent Lord, the Prince of Darkness.

      I have not spared myself in attempting to foment suspicion, ill-will, mistrust, and confusion wherever possible. However, up to now, I have been able to report only minimal success. I did achieve a falling-out between two old friends, Abigail Finch and Bertha Peters, by leading them to believe that each had tried to influence the judge of the cake-baking contest at the County Fair. I was also successful in convincing the banker Morton Bancroft to make a conspicuously large donation to the Fire Engine Fund, thereby stirring up some resentment and jealousy among the other leading citizens of the town. And I was able to persuade the proprietor of Tracey's Tavern to stay open one hour later every Saturday night.

Despite these achievements, I am well aware that all of this must look like penny ante stuff to those of you back at Headquarters.

What you fail to recognize, perhaps, is that these are simple folk here in Needmore. They just aren't susceptible to our truly venomous temptations. Dishonesty is rare among them; lechery is confined to the occasional reading of a racy novel; drunkenness is an affliction suffered only by the town wastrel, Harvey Benson, for whom they all feel an indulgent affection. The closest anybody comes to out-and-out hatred occurs when the umpire calls a close play against the town baseball team. In short, the people I've been assigned to corrupt are hopelessly, frustratingly, and monotonously *good*.

Your response to my last report, urging me to be more imaginative in my work, got me moving in the right direction, however. I asked myself, "What is the one sin that earthlings, regardless of how good they are, find irresistible?" And in a flash, the answer came to me — *greed*.

At last I had my overall aim! The next step was to develop a strategy and find a place to begin. Where had I observed even small traces of greed among the townspeople? I remembered hearing several boys at the Sunday school picnic complaining because there hadn't been more than one piece of cherry pie for everybody. I recalled that the owner of the feed store, Clarence Cratz, told his customers that unless profits picked up soon, he would be forced to go out of business. (When I checked it out, though, I discovered that Clarence has been saying the same thing every year since 1949.) I didn't have much to go on.

Then I remembered how the minister of the only church in town always shakes his head despairingly at the contents of the offering plate after Sunday worship. Here was a fertile field for the seeds of greed!

I began my campaign by directing Pastor Trimble's attention to an article in a clergy magazine. There he read about another minister who had come up with an interesting idea. Like many ministers, Trimble didn't much enjoy reading about ideas that worked elsewhere. From experience he knew they wouldn't work in his situation, but he felt obligated to try some of them anyway. . .just in case. That meant more work. It also meant disappointment when these experiments inevitably failed to live up to the success of the story in the professional journal.

But this particular story fired Trimble's imagination. The minister who had written the article explained that when the offering plate had been passed one Sunday morning, the worshipers were invited to take instead of give. Actually, they were borrowing for the purpose of using the money to make more money. When the returns came in several months later, the original fifty dollars had multiplied nearly four times.

It didn't take much encouragement to get Pastor Trimble started thinking big: "If fifty dollars brought in two hundred, why then a thousand would bring in four thousand, and five thousand could bring in *twenty thousand*! It would be a glorious, living illustration of the parable of the talents in the Gospel of Matthew."

Now, of course, I know we devils are not permitted to read the Bible, except for the purpose of misleading human creatures. And we must always secure special permission for doing so from the Bureau of Dispensations. However, time was of the essence in this case, so I snuck a quick look at the story. I recognized it from our study at training school as one of the parables of J – – – –. It's about this wealthy man who gives money to his servants, then goes on a journey, and expects a return on that money when he comes back. Very thought-provoking. Worthless trash, of course, but still, very thought-provoking.

And so while Pastor Trimble's thoughts went immediately to the good that all this money would accomplish, my own thoughts were spent in a delightful contemplation of the arguing and fighting the money would cause when it came in. One person would want it spent to put a new roof on the church. The music people would want a new organ. Someone else would want the money to go for missions. Still another person would no doubt suggest it be spent for a beautiful stained glass window. I could imagine at least twenty different projects that would be proposed. There's nothing quite like a large sum of unexpected money to get church people fighting!

I predict that soon the entire church, and then the whole town, will be involved. We can confidently anticipate such wonderful things as name-calling, angry accusations, even some honest to badness hatred.

With only a little encouragement from me, I'm sure Pastor Trimble will put up the $5,000 from his own life savings. With the anticipated four-fold return, that would leave $15,000 for everyone to fight over.

My next report to you will, undoubtedly, be of the huge success of this venture. I hope, Director, that I am not premature in requesting consideration for a promotion. Maybe I can use this same scheme at a higher level. What do you think?

Subversively yours,

Pharnum Groacher

How much time elapsed between the events noted in the previous document and those noted in the following cannot be determined precisely. The word "quarterly" does not necessarily refer to a three month period.

To: Ferule Flogmaster

From: Pharnum Groacher

Re: Fourth Quarterly Report

Dear Director:

Well, the best-laid plans of mice and men — and devils — sometimes go awry. Let me hasten to add that the failure really wasn't my fault.

As I had anticipated in my last report, Pastor Trimble decided to put up $5,000 of his personal savings for what he called the "Sharing God's Talents" project. What I didn't foresee was that he would talk the bank into lending him another $5,000. At first the project was publicized only in the local paper, but somehow word reached the big city newspapers, then the press services. Before you could say "Old Nick," Needmore was a celebrity town.

Soon the applications started pouring in. The church council made the decisions on who would get how much, and I can happily report that a great deal of wrangling took place in the process.

The biggest fight occurred when the church treasurer, Mary Farnsworth, pushed for a loan for her brother-in-law who said he would use the money to develop gasoline from watermelon rinds. He was positive, she said, that his new product would solve the country's ongoing need for a domestic energy source and net a tidy profit for the church as well. His request was denied, but not without arousing bitterness. Mary Farnsworth resigned as treasurer. Then I found out everyone had been hoping to get her out of that job for the last fifteen years. Oh well, we can't win them all.

Anyway, the council had a hard time deciding who would get the money. They finally approved fifty people to get loans ranging from $1 to $500. Then they settled back to wait for the returns.

The first indication of trouble came when a youngster who had borrowed a dollar to buy seeds for a vegetable garden claimed his dollar bill had accidentally been blown away by a sudden gust of wind. Then Dan Jaspers, who had been given $50, reported that he had been assured that "Lucky Dan" in the fourth race at Aqueduct was a sure thing, but. . . .

After that, the council members started getting nervous. They began contacting the folks who had so eagerly volunteered for "Sharing God's Talents." And they discovered, to their chagrin, that nearly half of those folks had given phony names and addresses. Those who *could* be reached, when they didn't offer lame excuses, were somewhat unhappy about being contacted. "Why don't you people get off my back?" was one of the milder responses.

When the final tally was in, only $1,500 of the original $10,000 had come back. In a tearful sermon to his flock, Pastor Trimble complained that, in the parable, even the *wicked* servant had at least returned what was originally given to him.

Of course, I personally regret the breakdown of my original scheme. On the other hand, the cheating and lying made possible by the borrowed money is a plus for our Cause. And the things they are saying around town about Pastor Trimble and the church

council are a delight to my fiendish ears. So, far from
viewing the whole project as a failure, I regard it as a
smashing success. I've managed to undermine confidence in the Bible and the church at one stroke, to
say nothing of proving beyond a shadow of a doubt the
potential for depravity in the human heart.

I think it not unfitting that my name be
included in the nominations for the "Temptation of the
Year" award. I realize that it is unusual for an agent on
probation to be considered for such a high honor, but,
in this case, you may want to make an exception.

Confidently yours,

Pharnum Groacher

To: Pharnum Groacher

From: Director Ferule Flogmaster

Re: Reassignment

You ninny! The very last thing we want humans
to become aware of is precisely what you boast about
bringing to their awareness: "the potential for depravity
in the human heart." Surely you know that our aim is
always to keep mortals smug and complacent, convinced of their own goodness. The minute they start
thinking otherwise, they do all sorts of dreadful things,
like asking for forgiveness, opening themselves to the
grace of Heaven, and experiencing the Adversary's
acceptance of them.

You were sent to Needmore merely to maintain the status quo, to keep the people happy in their good opinions of themselves as nice people.

Therefore, this is your official notice that we will indeed make an exception in your case. Instead of allowing you to continue in your present post, you are being reassigned immediately to the job of file clerk in our Records Bureau, where the worst your stupid bungling can accomplish is an occasional misplaced file folder.

F. F.

Groacher Takes On Higher Education

As should by now be obvious, Pharnum Groacher is not a very good devil. That may sound like an oxymoron: devils, after all, aren't supposed to be "good." To be more precise, then, Groacher is a bungler. Give him an A+ for effort because he does try — heavens, how he tries! — but he somehow manages to take a nearly hopeless situation and turn it into an absolutely hopeless situation, viewed, that is, from the standpoint of the Hades Home Office.

However, while Groacher is not exactly a whiz at the business of subversion and corruption, he is personally resourceful and unquenchably optimistic. These latter traits are exhibited fully in the opening lines of the following set of communications, most of which are personal letters to one Gordo Glummer, apparently a devil with whom Groacher had struck up an acquaintance during his assignment to the Records Bureau.

To: Gordo Glummer
         Bureau of Diabolic Records
         Dark Shades Drive
         Hades

From: Pharnum Groacher

Re: The situation in academia

Dear Gordo:

You still can't believe it, can you? I mean the clever ruse I pulled to get myself out of that dreary Records Bureau where you and I learned to know each other. What I don't understand is why you haven't managed to do the same. Why the delay? With the access you have to the files on field assignments, you can easily do what I did: find a position that looks attractive, type up the appropriate form, and then forge the fiend director's signature. I know it's risky, but I'm living proof that it can be done.

Sometimes I do envy our heavenly counterparts. Things like forgery, bribery, and blackmail are unheard of among them. So they have no security guards, no secret police, no spies trying to catch them in wrongdoing. Just think, Gordo, what you and I could get by with in Heaven!

As devils, of course, everyone expects us to be sneaky and devious and dishonest. Even so, I was amazed at all the restrictions they had in the Records Bureau. I still can't believe I got away with it! But here I am, seated in a comfortable room in the Longworth Dormitory. A bright devil like you would just love it here in academia. I promised in my last letter to tell you something about my duties in this place. So here goes.

Pondermore College is situated in a most unpleasant part of Pennsylvania. The campus has lots of large trees, green grass, duck ponds, ivy-covered buildings. Seems like the sun shines every day. Depressing. Fortunately, the temperature this time of year is deliciously hot — reminds me a little of home. Even more exciting are the delightful thunderstorms which sometimes roar through the town.

The work itself is the kind of challenge that appeals to me. I've been assigned to a group of sophomore students. Naturally, there's not as much prestige connected with this assignment as there is for agents placed in charge of the seniors, to say nothing of the faculty or the administration. But at least I'm a step above the poor slobs who have the freshmen to deal with. Before long, I am confident I can work my way up, maybe even to Pondermore's administrative council. I do think it would be wonderful to try my hand in the politics of "respectable" institutions. Unlike government politics, where everybody expects everybody else to be opportunists, the scheming and backstabbings at a

church-related college like Pondermore are carried out
under a cover of civilized respectability. It's the perfect
environment for that most delicious of all sins —
hypocrisy. But I digress.

Just now we are nearing the end of the summer
session, so things are kind of relaxed around here. I
don't have to work too hard keeping the students I'm
responsible for away from their studies. A whispered
suggestion or two in their ears, and they will decide to
go out drinking instead of hitting the books. There are
a few difficult cases — Danny, for example, who
actually goes to church on occasion. I sometimes have
a tough job convincing him that sleeping in on a
Sunday morning will do him more good than sitting
through a boring sermon. "You're going to sleep
anyway," I tell him. 'Why not do it in the comfort of
your bed? Besides, you worked hard on your account-
ing course this week. You deserve a break." That
usually convinces him.

The case I'm most enthusiastic about is Mark.
He comes from a prominent family. His father is president of his own corporation — one of those small elec-
tronic firms that has latched on to lucrative contracts
with the U.S. Defense Department. He serves on the
boards of several banks. Last year he headed the United
Way campaign, and for years he has been a prominent
member (meaning big contributor) of the status church
in his community.

Anyway, by the time Mark fell into my hands,
he had begun to question some of his father's values,
had experimented a little with grass, was making
earnest attempts to lose his virginity. . .the usual. Mark
is one of those loathsome young people who seem to
emerge in every school. He is bright, talented, good-
looking, athletic, and gregarious. If that weren't bad
enough, he manages to endear himself to everyone by

affecting a believable humility. I'm sure this humility isn't genuine; but even if it is, I am proceeding on the conviction that it can be subverted into its counterpart — full-blown pride.

As a Big Man on Campus, Mark is especially susceptible to the temptation of pride. I've been working hard on this while, at the same time, trying to accentuate some of his doubts about the beliefs and values he learned in his younger years. There is even a hint that he is beginning to reject the plan so dear to his father's heart that Mark will eventually take over the family business. I have encouraged Mark to read such old reliables as Voltaire and Nietzsche, plus some modern writings guaranteed to make him skeptical of the existence of the Adversary. I'm making progress on this front.

Yesterday I caught him laughing when his philosophy professor made a snide remark about "the so-called miracles mentioned in the Bible." I've managed to spice up Mark's vocabulary with some new profanities. All signs indicate that he is moving in the direction of agnosticism.

It's fun here, Gordo, it really is. Why don't you finagle a way to join me? We would make a great team.

Sincerely,

Pharnum

The next letter in the file was apparently sent several months later. Groacher is obviously still enthusiastic about his assignment, but he now has some concerns about his prize catch, Mark Rogers.

To: Gordo

From: Pharnum

Re: The latest developments at Pondermore

Dear Gordo,

Thanks for your recent letter. Sounds like things are changing down there in Records. I can see why the front office thinks a new computer system is the way to go. But really, machines have their limits. I suppose they are indispensable in terms of record keeping. But I do object to the recent pressure we field agents have been getting to utilize some of the new software packages designed for use with Christians. As far as I'm concerned, there is just no substitute for the personal demonic touch in the temptation and subversion game.

Take, for instance, some of the techniques I've been using here on my sophomore males. I figure the place to start is with the problems already on their minds. Once I know what's worrying them, I try to take advantage of that. For example, most of these guys have anxiety about grades. Some more than others, of course. Usually, the brighter a student is, the more anxiety he suffers. So I try to do two things at once. I encourage them to worry about exams and papers they must write, and at the same time I use every maneuver I can to get them to procrastinate. The object is to establish a nasty little pattern of behavior that will plague them throughout their lives. I want them to get caught in the frustrating snare of knowing they ought to be doing something but not being able to do it. This combination of guilt and anxiety works every time.

Usually they begin doubting themselves, then actively hating themselves. A magnificent, full-blown depression often follows.

Then there is loneliness. Combined with sexual frustration, it is a powerful tool in the hands of a master tempter like myself. It isn't hard to pull these students into self-pity. They have this image of the ideal male college student as bright and witty, surrounded by admiring friends and adoring co-eds. And yes, most of these guys have copies of *Playboy* or *Penthouse* magazine lying around. Contrary to what the puritans think, the damage done by such magazines has little to do with their pictures of nude women, although it is true I enjoy seeing my students building a mental picture of women as gorgeous creatures who desire little more than to give men sexual pleasure. As long as *Playboy* and its even raunchier cousins are willing to dehumanize women, and therefore men as well, all I can say is more power to them!

However, the real and, from our standpoint, most welcome effect such media produce (and that includes movies, television, and nearly all advertising) is the notion that the world and everything in it exists for their personal pleasure. To paraphrase what one of the American presidents once said, the message communicated by the so-called men's magazines is: ''Ask not what you can do for the world around you; ask rather what the world around you can do for you.''

These college guys get the message that the ideal man is urbane and sophisticated, with beautiful women longing to spend their nights with them. When they realize how far they are from fulfilling this image, they become anxious. Their sense of loneliness becomes exaggerated to the point of being all but unbearable. They begin feeling sorry for themselves. And yet they must never let anyone guess how bad they feel. So they keep up this phony front of being cool and "laid-back," as they put it. Here again my idea is to establish lasting patterns of behavior that will make their lives miserable. Self-pity and insecurity do wonders in helping mortals get hung up on materialism and status. One way to compensate for feeling bad about yourself is to acquire enough power or money to prove to yourself and others that you really are worth something. Isn't it great how so many earthlings fall into this trap?

So much for the good news. I must confess that I am a bit concerned about Mark Rogers. You remember my telling you about the progress I'd been making on his case? I was so sure he had the makings of an atheist. He was asking such pointed questions of his teachers, reading such provocative books, refusing to accept conventional solutions to both human problems and questions of faith.

But lately I've noticed some changes. As the French say, "cherchez la femme." There is a woman involved. She's a sweet young thing, and I'm afraid she's going to turn his head. Know any good strategies to prevent this, Gordo?

Cordially,

Pharnum

Next in the file is the reply Groacher received from his friend Gordo, but it is a long-winded, dull letter detailing the changes taking place in the Records Bureau. The next pertinent document in the file is Groacher's last communication from Pondermore College, written just before the surprise he received which marked an end to his time as a tempter assigned to college sophomores. This letter is unique in its pervasive pessimism. Groacher, for the first time, admits failure.

To: Gordo

From: Pharnum

Re: Rogers

Dear Gordo,

I have terrible news. There is no use trying to deceive myself any longer. I just don't have what it takes to be a competent devil.

You remember Mark Rogers, the prospect I was so excited about? Well, we've lost him — for good, I'm afraid. Even as I write, he is talking with Lisa, that wretched little flirt, about wedding plans. All my hard work is about to go down the drain. His enthusiasm for exploring radical ideas has been replaced by plans for finishing his college work as soon as possible in order to work for his father. And horror of horrors, he has begun attending church occasionally. He now describes his former questions about matters of faith as "immature." He wants to lead a comfortable, happily-married life.

Oh, Gordo, where have I failed? To have this skeptic turn into a believer is sure proof that I really am incompetent, just as my superiors have said. I've never felt so worthless.

Despondently yours,

Pharnum

The end of this episode comes in the form of an unexpected memo sent by the Director of the Pondermore College Task Force for Subversion of Students and Faculty.

To: Werner Wolfsbane, Superintendent
        Higher Education Division
        Madalyn Murray O'Hair Plaza
        Hades

From: G.D. Shamesworthy
        Director of the Pondermore College Task Force
        for Subversion of Students and Faculty

Re: Agent Groacher

Superintendent:

This memorandum is my personal recommendation that Agent Pharnum Groacher receive both a Citation of Outstanding Achievement and a promotion. His excellent work with Pondermore student Mark Rogers testifies to his ability to turn what looked like failure for our Cause into smashing success.

The Rogers case, as you know, was of grave concern to us. This popular and gifted student had influenced many of his fellow students in his concern for others. He had been active in efforts to organize his classmates to volunteer time in working with underprivileged children. Unwilling to accept the values and beliefs of his childhood, he was displaying a dangerous tendency to think for himself. By discarding the rigidity of traditional piety, he was well on the way to developing a strong, well-tested faith of his own. He was beginning to see that faith in J – – – – C – – – – – called for radical commitment of life, for putting beliefs into action.

But Agent Groacher saved the day! Somehow he persuaded the Rogers boy to settle instead for a comfortable, undemanding faith. Groacher apparently urged him to marry, go into his father's business, pursue an upwardly mobile life style, and forget all that nonsense about caring for those less fortunate than himself. Our latest investigation reveals that Rogers will undoubtedly drift into belief that the Adversary is a vaguely benevolent deity, nice to have around when one gets into trouble. In his remarkably subtle fashion, Groacher prevented Rogers from encountering the true Adversary, the active, loving Power who confounds so many of our efforts. Instead, Rogers will see religion as something one does on occasional Sunday mornings. Like so many others, he will make little connection between his comfortable Christianity and the human issues of the day. Thanks to Agent Groacher, a potentially menacing enemy has been reduced to a harmless, nominal Christian.

I am sending a copy of this communiqué to Groacher. I want him to know I'm proud to have been his Director. I wish him well in what will undoubtedly be a brilliant future.

Highest Regards,

Director G. D. Shamesworthy

Groacher Goes To Washington

In what he had mistakenly thought was his correspondence with a heavenly agent, Groacher had mentioned that a new policy in Hell called for demonic agents to be assigned not to individuals, but to groups. However, as evidenced in his work with the student Mark Rogers, Groacher, who was formally trained under the new policy, could not avoid zeroing in on one of his charges for some old-fashioned, individualized temptation. The enthusiastic response of Director Shamesworthy illustrates the serious political rift in the power circles of Hades.

Yes, such things do occur in the realm of Darkness — a fact which should elicit no surprise from informed readers. The seeds of such rebellion were sown in Heaven when Lucifer attempted his coup, as John Milton so brilliantly reported. It is therefore hardly shocking to discover that power struggles rage among Satan's minions.

The Sociological Approach, which has been official demonic policy for the past generation, still has not won the enthusiastic endorsement of all high-placed officials. A strong current of traditionalism continues to run through the murky waters of Hadesian politics.

Lately, a powerful, conservative movement has arisen. Its advocates are determined to force a return to the more traditional methods of temptation. Naturally, this movement is a clandestine one. Devils like G. D. Shamesworthy, whose vigorous endorsement of Groacher's handling of the Mark Rogers situation led him to recommend a promotion for Groacher, are obviously members of the conservative movement. It is also obvious that Superintendent Wolfsbane, to whom Shamesworthy's memo was addressed, shares the same ideology. Otherwise, Shamesworthy would never have used the phrase, "the Rogers case." To do so runs counter to new policy directives which demand that names of individual earthlings be used only when necessary for identification or in order to understand significant patterns of behavior. The fact that Groacher did indeed receive a promotion (as becomes evident in subsequent correspondence) underscores the fact that the Higher Education Division remains a stronghold of the underground conservative camp.

Not surprisingly, the official political structure of Hell is totalitarian. Once it came to power, the Freedom Party declared itself the only authorized party permitted to exist. Apparently the Freedom Party takes its name from that same cosmic event which Milton described with the words:

> Him [Lucifer] the Almighty Power
> Hurled headlong flaming from the ethereal sky,
> With hideous ruin and combustion, down
> To bottomless perdition; there to dwell
> In adamantine chains and penal fire,
> Who durst defy the Omnipotent to arms.*

Contrary to Milton's view, the inhabitants of Hades regard the "fall" from Heaven as something else altogether. They call it instead "The Glorious Rebellion." The honored participants in that ancient celestial struggle are still called the freedom fighters. Hence the name Freedom Party, although in ordinary demonic conversation this group is called simply "the liberals."

Groacher remains ignorant of all such political machinations. Basking in his promotion, he has no inkling that his Citation for Outstanding Achievement was given to him for political reasons. And, despite his rather striking list of failures, Groacher continues to think of himself as a talented demon whose true abilities have not yet been recognized. This is amply demonstrated in his first communication from Washington in a letter addressed to his old crony.

*ED. NOTE: from Paradise Lost, Book One by John Milton.

To: Gordo Glummer
        Bureau of Diabolic Records
        Dark Shades Drive
        Hades

From: Pharnum Groacher

Re: Assignment to Washington

Dear Gordo:

What's that old expression about the cream rising to the top? One thing I'll say for myself, Gordo, is that I've always believed my talents would finally come to the attention of the right demons. But even I can't believe my good fortune this time. Imagine, here I am in Washington, D.C., rubbing shoulders, so to speak, with senators and congressmen, generals and ambassadors. My assignment, as you may have heard, is to a Congressional sub-committee dealing with foreign policy matters.

Incidentally, Gordo, I know that some of my old classmates from Brimstone Training School days are spreading nasty rumors. They are saying that my out-standing work at Pondermore College was nothing but a colossal bit of luck. Needless to say, you know better. I can assure you that I'll soon be moving on to bigger and better things here in Washington. I have my sights set on an assignment over at State, as they call it here, or maybe even the National Security Council. Tell you what, Gordo, since you enjoy the administrative side of things, I'll use my influence to get you a post some-where in the General Services Administration. You wouldn't believe the bureaucratic red tape over there. (Or maybe you *would* believe it, since some of our top agents have had a hand in creating the mess there.) Anyway, you would have a great time spreading confusion and frustration. Let me know if you are interested.

> *Sincerely,*
>
> *Pharnum*

The next item of correspondence in the file is a report sent by Groacher to his superior, Malchus Gnashwell, describing his activities in his new post.

To: Supervisor Malchus Gnashwell
        U.S. Government Affairs Division
        Legislative Bureau
        Benedict Arnold Square
        Hades

From: Agent Groacher

Re: Initial Washington report

Dear Supervisor:

Following your excellent advice, I first of all studied the personality profiles of the earthlings entrusted to my care. My personal commendations to our Bureau of Personality Studies for this valuable background information. It is one of the best improvements brought about by yourself and your colleagues. It gives us a decided edge on the heavenly agents.

And speaking of heavenly agents, this place is crawling with them (or maybe ''fluttering'' with them would be more appropriate...please forgive my little jokes; I continue to find it hilarious that some mortals persist in picturing angels with wings and devils with pitchforks). Washington must, indeed, be an important place to justify Heaven's assignment of so many of its operatives to it. The competition is rough because the stakes are so high. Naturally, I am quite proud that I have been chosen to be among the many crack agents our side has commissioned to this place. Let me assure you, Supervisor, that I thrive on pressure situations.

Studying the personality profiles, I discovered that the earthlings assigned to me are highly competitive. They have to be, to get where they are. Most of them bring to their jobs an equal mix of shrewdness and ambition. And they work very hard. They fight hard and play hard, too. The pressures on them are intense and provide wonderful opportunities for the kind of subversion I specialize in.

My plan of attack is based on the undeniable fact that both the elected officials and the staff of the sub-committee on foreign policy are susceptible to the privileges of their status. They are used to having things go their way. They give an order to an underling and expect it to be carried out promptly and efficiently. They receive the fawning attention of people currying political favors of all kinds. Why not use all this to our advantage?

It shouldn't be hard to persuade these high-placed people that they are a special breed, able to rise above the weaknesses that plague the masses. I've been busy seeing to it that more and more temptations come their way. And it's working! For instance, learning of one congressman's weakness for alcohol, I have been encouraging him to think that he can handle it because of his superior will power. And I've led him to justify his drinking by telling himself that it helps him "unwind" from all the pressures he is under. I'm happy to report that he now has a serious drinking problem.

It's much the same with sexual temptation. To quote a former Secretary of State, a mortal whose high government position enabled many beautiful women to overlook his less-than-handsome physiognomy, "Power is the great aphrodisiac." Luckily for our Cause, the earthlings found this statement merely amusing. They failed to reckon with the truth of it, that power indeed attracts like a magnet. I've managed to get almost half of the committee and staff to succumb to this temptation.

Congressman Morgan is a good example. As a high school student he had ground his teeth in frustration as he saw the most attractive girls falling all over the sports heroes. With his thick glasses and a physique his best friend once described as "stubby," he was operating under an obvious handicap. In college his academic achievements and election to student government won him some respect from his peers, but the women he wanted to impress still kept their distance. He ended up marrying a rather plain, timid female who had gazed at him adoringly when he presided at meetings of the student senate. It was only when he began running for Congress that he began to notice something that startled and pleased him. Women were no longer turned off by his less-than-striking appearance. Now in his late thirties, he makes sure that he has the final decision in selecting the college interns who apply to his office. Inevitably, at least one of them will turn out to be a lovely female, and almost as inevitably, she will succumb to his sexual overtures. He excuses his behavior with the rather odd rationalization that his previous fidelity to his wife means he has "paid his dues," to use the phrase he frequently

mutters to himself on the way home from an amorous
liaison.

Less inclined to make excuses for her sexual
activity is one of the sub-committee's legal advisors.
Marla Swenson is single, ambitious, and a woman who
unapologetically describes herself as "hot-blooded." A
man who can vouch for this description with considerable delight is a congressman who has been the
beneficiary of her libidinal enthusiasm at least twice a
week for the past month. A large part of their passion
for each other stems from the business-like demeanor
they must affect toward each other on the job. Shedding
their clothes becomes a wild shedding of all the
restraints they must normally observe.

This happy state of affairs (if you will forgive a
bad pun) not only means the people involved in these
escapades are less effective in their work but also
opens up the possibility of scandal and even blackmail.
Sexual dalliance is overlooked at the highest levels of
human enterprise so long as one plays by the rules.
The primary rule is simple: "Be discreet." As a hand-
some senator with presidential aspirations ruefully discovered, having a public fling with a luscious young
blonde is a flouting of the rules that will not be
tolerated. Perhaps the best thing about that well-
publicized business was the wonderful flowering of
hypocrisy it made possible.

Sex surely ranks as one of the most glorious
gifts the Adversary gives to humans. But, as always, the
more glorious the gift, the more possibilities we have
for perverting it for our own uses. And what a splendid
job we have done in turning sex into a potent weapon.

But the big project I'm working on involves
greed. The chairman of the sub-committee, I've
learned, is susceptible to bribery. He has not yet taken
any money under the table, but he is definitely weaken-

ing. I keep planting in his mind the notion that all his hard work for his country has gone unrewarded financially. He is beginning to believe that he deserves a big payoff as compensation for his outstanding contributions as a public servant. He can't help comparing his own financial situation with that of some of his colleagues who are obviously more wealthy than he and possess far lesser abilities.

The battle in his mind is raging, and this alone has distracted him from his work. Soon I anticipate being able to report that he has accepted an illicit offer of more than $100,000 from one of the Arab governments. My colleague at the their embassy, Agent Dastard, assures me that the bribe will be forthcoming within the next few weeks. Once it has been transacted, we will bend every effort to arrange leaks to the news media.

With all hopes for this success and the public scandal sure to follow, I remain,

Confidentially yours,

Agent Pharnum Groacher

Other pieces of correspondence related to Groacher's stay in Washington are of no great significance: more boastful letters to his friend Glummer, Glummer's replies containing mostly gossip about people in the Records Bureau, several notes of encouragement to Groacher from his supervisor, Groacher's selections from the Temptation Tape of the Month Club, and the like.

By far the most interesting item is an official communiqué from none other than Grendel Grimgrinder, the ruthless boss of the Freedom Party. It is amazing simply because Grimgrinder and other party bigwigs usually work very hard at keeping their communications off the record. As with every totalitarian regime, the powers-that-be in Hell wish to give the illusion that the bureaucracy functions smoothly on its own, without interference from party bosses. I am at a loss to explain how Grimgrinder's memo made it into the Groacher file, especially since Groacher himself seems to be completely unaware of behind-the-scenes politics.

What makes this memo unique is Grimgrinder's extensive discussion of his party's philosophical viewpoint. Such writings rarely appear in anything but scholarly and theological treatises.

Incidentally, many are surprised to learn that theology exists at all in Hell. However, some reflection makes it perfectly understandable that theological study should hold a prominent place in academic circles of the nether world. How else can the denizens of Hell understand the strategies of Heaven than by earnest investigation of the evidence? While atheism is championed in Hell as an appropriate philosophy for mortals, it should go without saying that atheism is impossible for devils themselves. As the writer of the book of James understood, bringing someone to belief in the Adversary is hardly cause for celebration. "You believe that God is one," wrote the author of that epistle, "you do well." Then with devastating sarcasm he added, "Even the demons believe — and shudder." Give the demons credit at least for shuddering. That is a far more commendable response than the currently popular view of many people that God is a kind of indulgent grandfather. But I digress.

Give the demons credit also for more familiarity with the ways of Heaven than many humans can claim. Demonic agents are of necessity more familiar with the contents of the Bible than many believers. While clergy are often heard bemoaning the biblical illiteracy in their parishes, such a problem is unheard of among Groacher and his fellow-demons. In fact, some of the most brilliant biblical scholars and theologians anywhere can be found in Hell.

As I have already stated, it is most unusual that Grimgrinder's document should come into my possession. As Chairdemon of the Freedom Party, Grimgrinder has established a style of almost fanatical insistence that his considerable power be wielded covertly. He takes great care to remain behind the scenes, springing upon his enemies in the conservative camp with fearsome, unexpected attacks. The communiqué which follows, and takes the form of an innocent-looking memo, typifies Grimgrinder's style. It is obvious from the context of this missive that Pharnum Groacher himself has been blissfully unaware of the labyrinthine politics surrounding his career.

To: Malchus Gnashwell
        U.S. Government Affairs Division
        Legislative Bureau
        Benedict Arnold Square
        Hades

From: Grendel Grimgrinder
        Chairdemon, Freedom Party
        Moloch Circle
        Hades

Re: Agent Groacher

Gnashwell:

I'll get straight to the point. For some time now you have been under suspicion for certain counter revolutionary tendencies. Measures were taken to increase surveillance of your activities. The evidence has confirmed our suspicions. Effective immediately, you are relieved of your position and directed to report to Perdition Intelligence Agency headquarters for final disposition of your case.

So much for your orders. Naturally, I will not be present for your interrogation; appearances demand that I keep myself above such unpleasant details. I will be sorry to miss it. I should like to see the expression on your features when you hear the verdict and sentence pronounced. Since I will miss that delightful opportunity, I thought I would include in this friendly little note to you something of how we finally nailed you. Really, Gnashwell, I have come to expect more finesse from you and your reactionary cronies. Your handling of matters reveals that you are slipping.

I refer in particular to one Pharnum Groacher, one of the agents under your supervision. His reports to you revealed he was using methods totally in opposition to our new policies. He included particulars of his efforts to encourage what the earthlings refer to as "personal vices": such things as drunkenness, sexual promiscuity, and graft. Our field studies indicate that Groacher's goals were being achieved. Within a remarkably short time he had succeeded in creating enough disruption in the personal lives of the earthlings to which he was assigned so as to bring their work to a virtual standstill. What completely confounded us, of course, was Groacher's apparently sincere belief that he deserved to be congratulated for his efforts. Naturally, this all led to your doorstep. When we found your memos to him, urging him to keep up the good work, we had all the evidence we needed against you.

I find it hard to believe, Gnashwell, that a bright demon like yourself can seriously think that the old ideology will one day be back in favor. Surely by now the efficiency of the enlightened methods of our regime are obvious to all intelligent devils. Your methods have been convincingly discredited; the glory days of

celebrated individual sinners is long past. In this
modern era, we cannot afford the luxury of trying to
duplicate the successes of an earlier age: the likes of
Giovanni Casanova, Henry VIII, Catherine the Great
(what perfectly wonderful irony the earthlings occasionally come up with!), or John Wilkes Booth. To be
sure, they were deliciously evil characters, but we
cannot rely on their kind anymore.

Symbolic of the new era, of course, was the rise
to prominence of the Nazi regime in Germany. Yes,
their leader was the kind of monster we prize — one
who could mastermind the murder of millions while
privately showing great affection for schoolchildren and
dogs. But the beauty of the Nazi phenomenon was the
calm efficiency of a system that appealed to an order-
liness so often prized by the earthlings. What a stroke
of evil genius on our part to convince many "good"
Germans that they were simply obeying orders, that the
slaughter of innocents was somehow justified as a
service to the fatherland. Even more brilliant was the
strategy which convinced most people to blame the
Nazi juggernaut on one man — Adolf Hitler. Much as
Hitler himself made scapegoats of the Jews, the rest of
the world made Hitler and a few of his cronies the
scapegoats for the holocaust, an eventuality which
required the willing cooperation or, at the very least,
the refusal to face reality, of so many. Eliminate a few
bad apples, went the argument among "right-thinking"
people — get rid of a Hitler, a Himmler, an
Eichmann — and we can free ourselves of evil.

The nearly universal acceptance of this delusion
was perhaps our greatest victory ever. And it was the
overwhelming success of the strategy which produced
this victory that convinced demons like myself to
devote ourselves to the liberal cause. Within a short

time we purged the reactionaries from nearly every
position of leadership in Hades. Only a few die-hards
like you remain, and we will root you out one by one.

What I fail to understand is why you cannot see
that the cause of Satan, our Malevolent Lord, is best
served, not by tempting humans to a few petty (or even
gross) personal sins, but by turning them into unemo-
tional, calculating, efficient cogs in a bureaucratic
machine. Face it, Gnashwell, the effort spent in producing one drunkard is far better devoted to promoting a
social policy that will foist ruin and despair on an
entire population.

Take, for example, this sub-committee on foreign
policy to which Groacher was assigned. True, he succeeded in throwing the personal lives of its members
into turmoil. According to the old method, that would
have been considered commendable, perhaps even
worthy of promotion. But look what has happened.
The committee was well on its way to devising a plan
for increased sale of nuclear arms to several countries.
Think of the long term effects beneficial to our Cause
had that plan been carried out: human energy and
money diverted from productive activities into weapons
of destruction, an increase of international tension,
more fear at the increased threat of war, and finally, an
ongoing escalation of the arms race. All this could have
resulted if Groacher had simply urged the committee
members to study their charts and statistical tables
soberly, to make their decisions on a politically pragmatic basis, without regard to the flesh and blood they
share with all earthlings.

Our new methodology succeeds best with such
people if we can keep them isolated in their air-
conditioned offices, their chauffeured limousines, and
their country clubs. I need not remind you that one of
our most brilliant strokes of genius in dealing with

earthlings was to get their military warriors off the front lines of battle and into safe, comfortable war strategy rooms. The farther removed we got their generals from seeing the blood and smelling the stench of dying people, the better off we were.

The same principle applies elsewhere. By leading the earthlings into personal sin, Groacher made the fatal mistake of reminding them of their humanity, the same humanity which our Great Adversary sent the wretched Son to die for. It is very hard for mortals to be indifferent to the suffering of others when they have suffered themselves. What you and your co-conspirators still do not see, Gnashwell, is that one sin of indifference to human suffering is worth a hundred sins of personal vice.

Even some of the earthlings themselves understand what we are up to with our successful new policy. Some of the brightest Christian thinkers put their finger on it soon enough. Writing not long after Hitler's time, one of them observed:

> Modern man can no longer have confidence in the virtues of the individual, in his kindness, or his energy, because we are no longer confronted by individual sins but by the state of sin of humanity.*

It is unfortunate that thinkers like the earthling who wrote those words, Jacques Ellul, should have gotten on to us so quickly. As Ellul himself pointed out, however, the policy our party has espoused is not truly "new" so much as it is a return to the best tradition of Hell.

*ED. NOTE: from The Presence of the Kingdom by Jacques Ellul.

What the Christians stupidly call "original sin" is not really the story of one creature's disobedience. It is a statement describing a reality: the "solidarity of sin," to use an unfortunately precise phrase of Ellul. Or, as that contemptible Paul character put it, "there is none righteous, no not one."

What I simply cannot understand, Gnashwell, is why you and your cronies can't see this. Are you really that stupid?

Well, enough. You have your orders. See that you follow them promptly. As for Pharnum Groacher — well, I suspect that he was an innocent pawn in your game. Personally, I doubt he has the brains to be dangerous. Who knows? With some guidance, he might even turn out to be a half-decent agent. In fact, I like his consistently optimistic spirit. It's very close to what one might call a devil-may-care attitude.

May I suggest in closing that your only hope for leniency lies in naming your fellow-conspirators. Satan willing, we will one day be rid of all of you.

Implacably,

Grendel Grimgrinder

Groacher Versus Margaret Ames

The very title I have assigned to the next episode of Pharnum Groacher's career should alert the reader that Groacher has indeed remained ignorant of the ideological battle raging among his superiors in Hell. Ignorant, but also unconcerned. Groacher is simply not a political creature. Though he does not shrink from using whatever connections he has in order to advance himself — and he can stoop to bootlicking of the most abject variety when he thinks it is necessary — Groacher simply does not have the makeup of a conniving backstabber. For a demon, he is oddly good-natured. In his own way, he is a true innocent: trusting his pal Glummer with his private thoughts; assuming that his superiors have his best interests, as well as the greater interests of Hell, foremost in their thinking; even believing that good intentions will cover a multitude of job performance sins.

All these rather favorable assessments of Groacher's character are made, of course, from a humanistic standpoint, perhaps even a Judeo-Christian standpoint. Though Grendel Grimgrinder appeared somewhat charitable in his evaluation of Groacher, we must remember that he was writing a memo to his enemy. Grimgrinder, like all competent demons, is a master of the lie. His true opinion of Groacher simply cannot be determined from his memo to Malchus Gnashwell. In all likelihood Grimgrinder regards Groacher as incompetent enough not to pose a threat to himself or the liberal cause. Like most tyrants, Grimgrinder prefers inadequacy to brilliance in his subordinates.

It should come as no surprise, then, to learn that, as Groacher begins his new assignment, he commits the very ideological error that Grimgrinder railed against in the Gnashwell memo. Groacher focuses his attention, not on the organizational structure of the institution to which he is assigned, but on the individual who heads it. That is, he uses a personal approach, rather than taking the systems or structural approach advocated by the demons in power. Not that Groacher wasn't schooled in the proper methods. Earlier in his correspondence he testified to the instruction he received in "the sociological approach" at Brimstone Training School. What happened to Groacher is what happens to nearly everyone: in the day-to-day carrying out of duties, the lessons of the classroom invariably give way to the greater influence of personality traits. As incongruous as it may sound, Groacher is simply a "people demon."

The first item in this next installment is a letter from Groacher to his new supervisor.

To: Vulgas Ripkin
        Foundations Division
        Attila the Hun Plaza
        Hades

From: Pharnum Groacher

Re: New York assignment

Dear Supervisor:

What a thrill it is to get my first assignment to New York City, or "The Big Apple," as the earthlings call it. Could this be an example of their dark humor — choosing as a symbol for their city the very fruit which, according to popular notion, caused the downfall of Adam and Eve? After all, where else can one find such a delightful combination of slums, drug traffic, pornography, and violence of every kind? Walking down 42nd Street and looking at the empty, dissipated faces almost makes me feel at home. Such degradation, such filth. I love New York!

I want you to know, Supervisor, that I fully intend to use my varied talents to help keep this city a showcase for the power of our Malevolent Lord. That's why I'm so grateful for my appointment. It's a big responsibility to be assigned to the Warren Foundation for Humanitarian Activities. As you know, foundations such as this are invariably set up by successful businessmen who have spent their lives ripping off the public and underpaying their employees. Retired and sitting on the pile of money they've made, they get to feeling guilty for the methods they've employed to earn their lucre. Naturally, we demons try to promote guilt feelings whenever we can, because guilt usually leads to self-hatred, and self-hatred is the source of a hundred wonderful sins.

But guilt in the case of a multi-millionaire often leads him to suppose he can buy his way out of his guilt. That is an illusion, as we know, but the money he lays out trying to do so often produces unfortunate blessings to his fellow earthlings. The libraries built by Andrew Carnegie come to mind, for example. It is impossible to assess the damage done to our Cause by the learning all those books made possible. But perhaps the best — or, more accurately, the worst — example is Alfred Nobel, a munitions manufacturer whose products, when employed as military weapons, maimed and destroyed thousands. Guilt drove him to establish awards for human achievement and especially for peace. Ever since, our side has been trying to subvert these much publicized awards, but we have made all too little progress.

So I'm overjoyed at the chance to handle the Warren Foundation assignment. Here are millions of invested dollars being used to benefit humanity. Under my influence, I'm confident these funds can be diverted to projects that will serve our Cause instead of the Adversary's. I plan to concentrate my efforts on influential members of the board and, in particular, on the female who is its chairman. Her name is Margaret Ames, and she has made her mark on Wall Street. That's about all I know about her. I'll work up a dossier on her soon and send it into our Personality Profile Bureau.

I must confess, I haven't spent much of my career as an agent dealing with females in positions of power. But you know how females are — overly emotional, suggestible, easily led. I'm sure it won't be hard to get her into our camp. She is, after all, a daughter of Eve, and we all know how that female gave us the first foothold on Earth! With the chairman of the foundation board under control, it will be an easy matter to have the Warren Foundation serving the cause of His Satanic Majesty.

> *In His Service*
> *and*
> *Optimistically Yours,*
>
> *Pharnum Groacher*

What Groacher didn't know when he wrote this letter, and what he learned to his painful surprise, was that a bureaucratic shuffle had given him a new supervisor, an up and coming female demon onto whose desk his letter arrived. Without delay she dashed off the following memo.

To: Agent Groacher

From: Synica Snidemuller
       Supervisor of Agents Assigned to Foundations

Re: Your New York report

Groacher:

I'll get right to the point. As your new supervisor, I will not tolerate the blatant sexism contained in your last report. It's all very well to promote prejudice of every kind in earthlings. Racism and chauvinism add to the brokenness of the human family, a brokenness we must encourage in every way. Nevertheless, I learned very early that you male demonic agents make the human version of sexism seem almost saintly by comparison. I was willing to overlook some of your sexist language, your use of the word "business_men_," for example. Or, even worse, your reference to a female as "chair_man_" of the board. I was even willing to assume that it was merely ignorance, or possibly stupidity, that led you to use the pronoun "he" in reference to a generic use of the term "millionaire." Only a dolt would ignore the undeniable fact that there are numerous millionaires of the feminine gender. Far less forgivable was your idiotic interpretation of the biblical account of what the Christians call "the fall." Even they have moved beyond the traditional idea that Eve was to blame for the mess the world is in. You obviously were gone from B. T. S. before Tribula Nettles joined the faculty. Her course on biblical hermeneutics has done wonders in rooting out the kind of primitive thinking you exhibit.

All these annoyances on my part paled, however, when I read your description of Margaret Ames as "emotional, suggestible, easily led." What kind of Neanderthal brain lodges in that head of yours, Agent Groacher? I can only assume that, since I am female, your attitude toward me is in keeping with your estimation of Ms. Ames. I can guarantee you that I am neither overly emotional nor suggestible nor easily led. I can also guarantee that should I come across any further references to females even vaguely like the phrases used in your last report, I will pull you out of

that assignment so fast it will scorch your scrofulous
skin. I trust I have made myself sufficiently clear.

S. Snidemuller

*Groacher's reply to this memo includes several pages of abject
apology and assurance that his report had included sexist language
and negative comments about women only because he knew that
his previous supervisor, Vulgas Ripkin, quite unlike himself, was
a notorious male chauvinist. Groacher's apologies and flattery are
sickening in the extreme. I have chosen to spare readers that section
of his letter. Instead, I pick it up where he begins to describe his
plans for dealing with the head of the Warren Foundation's board.*

. . . As for Chair<u>person</u> Ames [*ED. NOTE: person
is underlined in the original*], I have obtained information about her which I intend to act on immediately.
Beyond such factual data as her age (45), her health
(generally good but occasional problems with allergies),
and her marital status (recently divorced after 22 years
of marriage), I have learned that some events in her
personal life are having a significant effect on her. First
was the death of her only sister just two months ago
from cancer. Although the two sisters had not been
especially close when they were growing up, they had
in recent years become each other's best friend. Phyllis
(the older sister) had been particularly understanding
and supportive while Margaret Ames was dealing with
the end of her marriage. Then, when Phyllis was
stricken with cancer, it was Margaret's turn to be the
helper.

Incidentally, Supervisor, I am not among those
who think that disease is an out-moded technique. I
believe it is still one of our best weapons, especially

now that we have introduced some brand new ones.
The AIDS phenomenon supports my view. Oh, I know
there are many in Hadesian scholarly circles who
believe that, since earthlings are finding cures to
disease, our primary demonic efforts should be shifted
to other areas. And one way to look at it is to assume
we have lost valuable ground. How much easier we had
it, goes the argument, when people believed that most
disease was really demonic possession, when lovely
epidemics wiped out entire populations.

But isn't it better the way it is now? Instead of
disease threatening humanity (doubtless they will come
up with a solution to the AIDS problem before long),
we've got the earthlings in a situation where they
themselves are the chief threat to their existence. With
nuclear weapons capable of reducing their planet to a
gigantic cinder, they never suspect we are behind the
whole thing. They hate and fear each other; and, in the
long run, that's a plus for our side.

As for disease, I think we have an advantage
now. It used to be that diseases struck quickly and
carried off the victims just as quickly. (Except for tuber-
culosis, of course. It was such a shame when we lost
TB as a major killer.) But, generally, it is better to have
sick people linger a long time. Illness gradually wears
down the spirit of the victim — though there are excep-
tions, of course — and the effect on the loved ones of
the victim is especially delightful. By turns, they feel
guilty, angry, depressed, and helpless. What more
could we ask?

Though I seldom take sides in ideological
debate, I must admit that the new thinking which
devised what the earthlings are calling "the AIDS
epidemic" was truly satanically inspired. Whether the
advantages AIDS has given us are of short or long
duration, the whole enterprise has doubtless succeeded

beyond our wildest hopes. We've got some humans attributing AIDS to the Adversary as punishment for gays. What a coup to have them thinking that Heaven and not Hell is the source of their plight! And when was the last time we had a disease going for us that was both communicable *and* resulted in a long, slow dying? AIDS is even better than TB because AIDS embroils the humans in controversy over sexual behavior instead of uniting them to fight the disease. We've got them disputing not only the whole issue of homosexuality itself, but also the issue of sex education of young people and the role of government in dealing with the problem. In short, we have advantages with this disease that we have never had before, with the possible exception of that glorious time when the bubonic plague ran amok. The fear and distrust AIDS has fostered is almost without parallel.

True, the disease has cut into some of the gains we could count on from casual sex and the resulting dehumanization which that practice produced, but, like so many other endeavors, demonic subversion of the earthlings involves trade-offs. Our loss in the area of promiscuity has been more than compensated for by the increase in suspicion, hostility, and even panic. Anything which keeps humans fearful of reaching out to each other is a plus for our side. And unlike nearly any other disease we have going for us, the victims of AIDS are frequently regarded with loathing rather than compassion.

But how far I have strayed from my subject, Margaret Ames! Please overlook my occasional digressions, Supervisor. I include them only to help you understand my working style more fully. And, since one of the primary interests supported by the Warren Foundation is medical research, I think my reflections have been somewhat relevant to my assignment.

To return to <u>Ms.</u> Ames [*ED. NOTE: Ms. is also underlined in the original*], I believe she is in a perfect frame of mind for my efforts to have best effect. In addition to the strain she has been under during her sister's illness, she learned just last week that her son has been on drugs and wants to drop out of college. So Margaret Ames is feeling a great many losses in her life. And, best of all, she has begun to doubt.

I thought you might be interested in reading an extract from her journal, Supervisor. I enclose only what I see as the pertinent passages.

> More than I have in a long time, I've begun to doubt myself. I can hardly believe that once upon a fairy tale time, I thought of myself as a good wife, an attractive woman. I used to think I was a good mother to my son. Obviously, that was an illusion too. And I used to think I was a loving, caring person. An outsider looking on would say that I was wonderful with my sister, Phyllis, in her last weeks — I went to visit her every day, talked with her, held her hand. But what an outsider would never guess is that I was doing all that for myself. It was my need that motivated me, not my sister's. And so now I doubt not only my own strength, but my image of myself as a giving person as well. Has all of it been self-deception?

> And where is God in all of this? Has God been the greatest deception of all? Phyllis never doubted God's love. And look at her reward: a lingering, painful dying. Can I believe in God in such a world? And if there is no point to human goodness — if God doesn't care about it one way or the other, or if there is no God to care about it — then what is the point of my work? Why devote myself to the cause of bettering society if, in

an ultimate sense, it simply doesn't matter?
We prayed for Phyllis to get well, and she
died. And now I cannot pray at all. If only
there was some sign, some hard, indis-
putable evidence that there is a reason, a
trustworthy pattern to all this. If only I could
know...

There you have it, Supervisor. I'm sure you will
agree that I ought to concentrate on solidifying the
doubts that have emerged in Margaret Ames. Her work
up to now as chair<u>person</u> of the Warren Foundation
Board has provided great benefit to the Adversary's
cause. Here is a chance to destroy that advance. We
intend, in particular, to encourage one of the new
board members to pursue a relationship with Margaret
Ames. His name is Arthur Waldmeyer, and the data on
him indicate that he is an agnostic who had a Jewish
father and a Christian mother, neither of whom, thank
Satan, was devout. They deliberately kept their son
from getting a religious education because they wanted
him to "make up his own mind." We have used this
ploy on parents many times, and it hardly ever fails.
Anyway, I'm sure his influence on Margaret Ames can
only help our interests.

Humbly,

Pharnum Groacher

*The next pertinent item in the file is another memo to Groacher
from Synica Snidemuller. The tone of her memo is more conciliatory
than previously. She includes some advice near the end of the
memo.*

> . . . As to Ms. Ames, Agent Groacher, a word of
> caution is in order. Don't rely too heavily on doubt as a
> strategy. Experience has taught us that doubt is
> remarkably volatile. To quote one of the earthlings'
> poets, one Alfred Tennyson:
>
> > There lives more faith in honest doubt,
> > Believe me, than in half the creeds.*
>
> Unfortunately for us, that observation, though
> doubtlessly exaggerated, has proved true all too often.
> Also unfortunate, despite the fact that the execrable
> Martin Luther believed the book of James should not
> have been part of The New Testament, is the inclusion
> of that book in the Christian scriptures. You may
> remember from your biblical studies curriculum that
> James warned: "faith without works is dead." Another
> memorable line runs: "I by my works will show you
> my faith." With these words the book of James was
> warning against overemphasizing the importance of
> belief. In this case, it is a warning you will do well to
> heed yourself.
> > Thus, I am suspicious of this Arthur Waldmeyer
> person you mentioned in your report. Yes, it is well
> that he is an unbeliever. But if he is the kind of person
> who has the capacity to love Margaret Ames, we could
> be in trouble. While belief rarely leads to love, the

ED. NOTE: from "In Memoriam, Part XCV" by Alfred Tennyson.

converse, regrettably, is not true. Love very often leads
to belief. Or rather, to faith. And I need not remind you
what an abomination true faith is.

My advice to you, Groacher, is to isolate
Margaret Ames. Keep her alone and feeling sorry for
herself. I do wish Headquarters would recognize the
limitations of you male demons in dealing with female
earthlings. They simply outclass you in so many ways.

S. Snidemuller

*The final document related to this episode is an urgent letter from
Groacher to his old friend Gordo Glummer. In it, Groacher urges
Glummer to pass along a report to his former supervisor, Vulgas
Ripkin. Groacher complains that he fears making the report to
Supervisor Snidemuller because "she is a male-demon hater and
wants to get me canned." He appeals to Ripkin to pull some strings
on his behalf. He then goes on to report that Margaret Ames has
won admiration from members of the Warren Foundation Board
for her decisive and brilliant leadership and that she has recently
received a citation from the White House hailing her as "a person
of exceptional wisdom and remarkable compassion."*

*Groacher blames this turn of events on the interference of Super-
visor Snidemuller. I include here only the last section of Groacher's
report to Vulgas Ripkin.*

...I can hardly be held responsible for losing Margaret Ames when my efforts were constantly being undermined by my superior. Furthermore, there was no way I could know that Arthur Waldmeyer's interest in Margaret Ames would blossom into the most disgusting kind of genuine love. As evidence that events beyond my control entered the picture, I enclose a pertinent excerpt from the journal of Margaret Ames:

> One of the best things Arthur has given me is the encouragement not to abandon my faith. How strange that it should come from one who is not himself a believer! He tells me that my faith is far more important to me than I recognize, that it is connected to every part of my life and work. The other night he said something I cannot get out of my mind: "It's all right to doubt, but don't forget to doubt your doubts."

> And so when I picked up the Gospels again — something I hadn't done for months — how ironic that I should immediately come upon the story of the man who, when Jesus told him "All things are possible to him who believes," burst out, "I believe; help my unbelief." That is exactly my own prayer now.

> I was reminded of that dream the priest had in *Monsignor Quixote*, a novel by one of my favorite writers, Graham Greene. I actually went and dug out the passage. In the dream, Christ had been saved from the Cross by a legion of angels. No final agony, no heavy stone to be rolled away, no discovery of an empty tomb. Writes Greene:

"There was no ambiguity, no room
for doubt and no room for faith at all.
The whole world knew with certainty
that Christ was the Son of God."

That dream was a nightmare for the priest.
And I understand why. I remember when
Phyllis was dying that part of me wanted her
to get angry at God. I wonder now if her
refusal to do so was her way of trying to
protect me. What she didn't understand was
that without doubt, faith isn't possible.
That's what I must remember as I try to help
my son put his life together, as I meet successes and failures every day at work, as I
allow myself to risk getting close to someone
like Arthur.

Lord, I do believe. But help my unbelief.

Supervisor Ripkin, I trust you will use your
considerable influence to assign blame for this sad turn
of events to the place where it belongs — your
incompetent successor, Synica Snidemuller.

Faithfully yours,

Pharnum Groacher

Groacher Enters
The Peace Movement

How does Pharnum Groacher receive his new assignments? More to the point, how does he manage to keep getting assigned to posts of major significance?

Available information on this question is sketchy, at best. There is always risk involved when attempting to read between the lines, but it does appear that Groacher's good fortune in assignments can be attributed, in large part, to sheer chance. Despite constantly botching one job after another, Groacher somehow manages to come out looking as if the failures were not his fault. In the Margaret Ames case, he managed to appeal to the right demon, going over the head of his supervisor, Synica Snidemuller, to his former boss, Vulgas Ripkin. But this success in "playing politics" seems much more a matter of luck than of a carefully calculated move on Groacher's part.

Groacher's very ingenuousness in political matters seems to be a plus as far as his career is concerned. Even his worst enemy could hardly accuse Groacher of being a conniving power grabber. In fact, while it is true that he has fallen afoul of several of his superiors along the way (Ferule Flogmaster, the director of Agents on Proba-tion; and the afore-mentioned Snidemuller, for instance), it is hard to identify any real enemies Groacher has, at least in the sense of his fellow-demons possessing the kind of implacable hatred enemies usually exhibit. Groacher's incompetence may cause annoyance or irritation or even exasperation on the part of his superiors, but not hatred. To most of his colleagues, Groacher comes across as good-natured and not very bright, certainly not the kind of demon who represents a threat to their own power. Groacher's checkered career has hardly been the kind to elicit envy. And so, in an atmosphere poisonous with plotting, blackmail, and backstabbing, Groacher seems to wend his way blithely along, much like a child walking through a snakepit, mysteriously protected by an aura of innocence.

There is always the possibility, of course, that Groacher's "innocence" is really a deviously clever disguise on his part. Given the sharp noses of his associates for detecting the odors of dis-sembling of any kind, however, it is most unlikely that Groacher could pull off such a deception.

Finally, it should be noted that Groacher's less-than-brilliant-record cannot be attributed solely to his own incompetence. Even his most demanding supervisors recognize that the influence of the Other Side, as they call it, must always be taken into account. Though they seldom acknowledge it publicly, the minions of Satan are all too aware that their efforts are combated at every turn by an opposing force. They recognize that their enemy specializes in snatching victory from the jaws of defeat, to use a phrase that originated with the biblical account of Daniel's celebrated escape from the den of lions, but applies even more dramatically to the Resurrection. (That event, incidentally, is never mentioned by name in Hell. When it must unavoidably be alluded to — by historians and theologians — it is referred to as "The Abomination.")

It would be inaccurate to say that Groacher's supervisors have been "charitable" in their response to his lack of success. Charity does not exist in their circles. Rather, they are simply resigned to the fact that even their most expert agents will be stymied in their nefarious schemes. With Groacher, the reverse of the biblical maxim seems to apply: "To whom little is given, little will be required."*

It may have been with such an attitude of low expectations that Groacher was assigned to People United for Peace (PUP), an organization of social activists. Once again Groacher's apparent innocence is exposed: he naively assumes that his former supervisor Ripkin has taken on the role of his patron.

---

*ED. NOTE: adapted from Luke 12:48: "To whom much is given...much will be required."

To: Vulgas Ripkin, Associate Executive
         Personnel and Assignments Bureau
         Pandemonium Place
         Hades

From: Pharnum Groacher

Re: My recent transfer

Dear Former Supervisor:

Imagine what a thrill it was for me to learn of your promotion to a new position. And what a position: a real "plum," as the earthlings put it! Of course, I know very little about your work in the past, but what I learned about your brilliant strategies while you were heading the Foundations Division convinced me that you would soon find a post worthy of your superior abilities. The shambles that division has suffered under your successor Snidemuller made it quite a relief for me to be transferred out from under her snippy remarks to my new assignment.

I am proud to be one of your ardent supporters. In fact, I hope you will not be offended to learn that I count myself your protégé. Many thanks for what I am sure was your firm hand in finding me a place here in the Self-Interest Group Commission. Although you will no longer receive formal reports from me, I thought you might be interested to learn of my work here. I fully intend to conduct myself in a way that will justify your confidence in me.

I'm delighted with the *name* of the commission I have been assigned to. Isn't it a delicious joke to take the earthlings' oh-so-serious designation of what they call "interest groups" and give them what we know to be their proper label: *self*-interest groups! A good example is an organization which, I must confess, I would have *loved* being assigned to: the National Rifle Association. With utmost solemnity, they insist that their organization has only the welfare of society at heart. We know, of course, that what they really want is a socially respectable excuse to carry around all those guns. What fun it would have been to see to it that this self-deception got translated into the bloodshed and anguish which guns make possible. Perhaps some day I will have such an opportunity.

My new appointment, of course, is not nearly so glamorous as working with one of the exciting hate groups would be. I would much prefer being assigned to the KKK or some left or right wing terrorist organization. The possibilities for mayhem are so volcanically great in those situations. However, I intend to make the best of my present assignment. People United for Peace (PUP) is a new, only recently prominent group of social activists. At present, I am engaged in studying the records of this group and getting acquainted with its leaders. From what I have learned so far, they appear to be a very earnest bunch, committed to world peace. It will be a formidable challenge to subvert their efforts, but one I have no doubt I am equal to.

Again, my sincere thanks for your efforts on my behalf.

Appreciatively yours,

Pharnum Groacher

One of the difficulties in sorting through the material in the Groacher file is the lack of dating on correspondence. Since time, as we experience it, does not apply to the denizens of Hell, the absence of dates is understandable, but frustrating nonetheless. The reader must depend upon internal evidence to determine proper sequence. It is not clear if the next document was written before or after the previous one. In any case, it obviously was submitted near the beginning of Groacher's assignment to PUP.

To: Supervisor Verruca Smutch
         Self-Interest Group Division
         Anathema Circle
         Hades

From: Agent Groacher

Re: Initial report

Dear Supervisor:

I would like to begin by letting you know how happy I am to be working under your supervision. In my only previous experience with a female director, I learned so much! I'm sure your vast knowledge of self-interest groups will be a valuable supplement to the skills I bring with me to this new assignment.

Permit me to outline the plan of attack I have prepared. As I have been studying our records on the methods used by PUP and giving special attention to key individuals in the organization, I have already reached some important conclusions.

1. THEY ARE WELL ORGANIZED. Within little more than a year of earth-time, PUP has become recognized as one of the leading social activist groups in the U.S.A. As I write, plans are underway to

establish chapters in several European countries. The small staff of PUP has done a remarkable job in getting wide-spread press coverage. Although PUP is not yet a household word, its p.r. people are busy spreading the word on PUP's latest scheme: one of those pseudo events that go over so well on television. They have chosen a Saturday in October for volunteers to spread out on football fields all across the country, forming the shape of a dove of peace carrying an olive branch in its beak. The demonstrations will take place at the half-times of college football games. Participants will dress in white (except for the olive branch people in green and the beak people in yellow). Hundreds of real doves will be released into the air. Goodyear blimps covering the major college games will flash the festivities to home viewers.

How was all this accomplished? Obviously, it didn't happen by contacting every university in the country. Instead, PUP planners used their connection with the president of just one university whose football team was scheduled for network coverage. When he bought the idea as a great way to get publicity for his school, PUP brought pressure on a few other well-known universities to fall in line. You know how eager the earthlings are not to be left behind on stunts like this.

There is a good chance that the President will be flown in by helicopter to make an appearance at the game between Notre Dame and UCLA. Naturally, he thinks the idea is stupid, but if voters believe it's a terrific thing, he'll be there. So what if the President has proposed a record high figure for military spending? He can always call it his ''Peace Dove Package'' and use the whole PUP idea for his own purposes. (Our agents have been behind such ploys for so long you would think the earthlings would have caught on by this time.

Luckily for us, they insist on supposing these political gimmicks are their own ideas.)

At any rate, this Peace Dove Day event illustrates what a disturbingly successful job the PUP planners are capable of. *My top priority in subverting PUP, therefore, is to disrupt and sabotage their organizing capacity.* Thus far, PUP planners have been remarkably unified in their approach to strategy. By sowing discord in the form of envy, mistrust, and power struggles among PUP staff and members of the board of directors, I am confident my goal can be achieved.

2. THEY ARE ABSOLUTELY CONVINCED OF THE RIGHTNESS OF THEIR CAUSE. Rarely have I seen a group so single-minded in their philosophy. They believe that nuclear disarmament is the only hope for human survival. Beyond a shadow of a doubt, they believe their efforts for peace are the last chance the world will have to escape the terrors of a nuclear holocaust.

As a result, they are extremely zealous, willing to put in long hours and to endure difficult working conditions. This is true both of paid staff and volunteers. Salary levels at PUP are low compared to similar positions in business and even in other social activist organizations. In fact, staff members seem to take a perverse sort of pride in the low salaries they receive, almost as if being underpaid proves how dedicated they are to the cause. Those who volunteer their time for PUP are no less zealous than the staff. If anything, they are more willing to sacrifice personal comfort for the cause, attending innumerable meetings, traveling at their own expense to conferences and training sessions, giving up many of their free evenings and weekends, and making large financial contributions.

All this has convinced me that *the second prong of my attack will be to undermine the strong convictions*

PUP members have about the truth of their political and moral positions. The best way to defuse zeal of any kind is to introduce the possibility that the chosen course just might be wrong, or at least a bit flawed. I will concentrate my efforts on a few of the most charismatic leaders and well-respected thinkers of the group. George Wright, for instance, has made his mark as a scholar and writer of repute. An Ivy League faculty member, he once served on the staff of a U.S. senator who was a firm advocate of increased military expenditures. George Wright's disillusionment with the collusion between the government and military contractors, and the resultant waste and corruption, led him to write a book on the subject and to become one of PUP's founders. From the outset, his celebrity status has been one of the best things PUP has going for it.

According to our dossier on him, Wright has lately been experiencing some marital difficulties, as well as health problems. He is ripe for a time of wondering if he has gotten carried away with his conversion to the peace position. I'll be encouraging him to dig out some of the authors whose dialectics influenced him early in his studies: Hegel, Kierkegaard, Tillich. He is ripe for a siege of remembering that intellectual "fair play" includes giving due consideration to all sides of an issue. Once he begins putting such ideas into speeches and writings, the debate on the issue of "truth" will spread like wildfire through the top ranks of PUP. Such debate will bring to the surface the personality conflicts that thus far have remained hidden. (For instance, I've learned that Alice Chambers, another of PUP's founders, has lately been feeling envious of Wright's celebrity status.) Soon after this kind of personal animosity emerges, we can count on some exquisitely nasty infighting breaking out. This will cause rank and file members to take sides, and then we can sit back and watch PUP disintegrate. Its influence will have been effectively destroyed.

Well, Supervisor, that is my strategy. Although I have given careful attention to all aspects of the situation, there may be one or two details I have neglected. I welcome any suggestions you have for fine-tuning what I have outlined.

Yours truly,

Pharnum Groacher

Unlike many high-placed demons, Groacher's new supervisor, Verruca Smutch, prefers to use the format of personal letter rather than memo or communiqué when dealing with the agents under her supervision. She even addresses them on a first-name basis. While both these practices represent a departure from Hadesian protocol, they are actually part of her management style. By affecting what can best be described as a "grandmotherly" attitude toward her subordinates, she apparently manages to make them believe she has their welfare at heart. Readers should not be surprised that such clever deception has an important place in the internal workings of Hell. In an atmosphere where the art of the lie has achieved near perfection, it is only to be expected that its practitioners cannot resist honing their skills on each other.

From the Desk of Verruca

My dear Pharnum:

Believe me when I say how much I appreciated your invitation to make suggestions for "fine-tuning" your strategy in regard to the People United for Peace organization. Since my job of supervising field agents demands constant surveillance of their methods and performance, an openness to receiving direction such as you exhibit makes my task so much easier. Be assured that whatever suggestions I make are intended to ensure the success of the enterprise on which you have embarked. If I occasionally recommend a strategy different from one you have projected, please do not regard it as a personal criticism. Instead, think of it as my lending you the benefit of my considerable experience. I have always taken special interest in the progress of the agents assigned to my care, especially those who are still at the neophyte stage. I want you to know I will be giving personal attention to your work, Pharnum. I believe strongly in a team concept for our Division. In other words, if you succeed, I succeed. We all succeed together.

With this little preface to my remarks, let me make some observations about the contents of your report. You are right on the mark when you describe PUP as well organized. Indeed they are. And you should do your best to see they *continue* to be well organized. Yes, I realize this advice may come as something of a surprise to you. Your assessment that "Peace Dove Day illustrates what a disturbingly successful job the PUP planners are capable of" is absolutely correct. And while your first reaction to the enormous interest in world peace which this event is generating may be to gnash your teeth, it is precisely to the success of this event that you must bend every effort.

"Why?" you ask. There are two answers to this question, and both of them are predicated on what I call the "big picture" theory. I hope you will not think me unkind, dear Pharnum, when I say that you have fallen into an error common to inexperienced agents. You have mistakenly pursued short term rather than long term objectives.

Let me illustrate. Obviously, it is not the will of our Lord Satan that nations live at peace. War continues to be one of our best weapons to thwart the designs of Heaven. While earthlings profess an abhorrence of war, they do so mostly because they are repelled by the spectre of death. They think of war mostly in terms of soldiers and civilians dying. They, too, take a short term view. They forget about the long term effects of war, all those wonderful horrors which plague the survivors of war: a lifetime of grief for lost loved ones, the bitterness of veterans who feel their sacrifice was not appreciated, broken bodies, broken dreams, destroyed national economies. . .the list could go on and on.

What some of our own agents (and, regrettably, even some of our leading strategists) do not realize is that the *threat* of war serves our purposes almost as well as war itself. Consider the cost of preparing for war. One of our great successes has been to persuade the earthlings that money for "national security" — don't you love the humans' proclivity for self-deceiving euphemism? — is well spent. Reports from the Bureau of Records continue to show that earthlings are spending well over two billion dollars per day for war or preparation for war. Per *day!* Our best interests are served by hiding the implications of that figure from their consciousness. Think what a loss it would be for our unholy Cause if those vast sums were spent instead to combat illiteracy, poverty, crime. Should the earthlings ever "beat their swords into plowshares" in the form of school buildings, housing for the poor, tools for medical research, and nameless other abominations, we may as well throw in the towel. Plainly, then, we must do all we can to subvert any real movement toward world peace.

The essential question, of course, is how best to accomplish this objective. Here is where the "big picture" theory comes into play. We must constantly ask: will this strategy, *in the long run*, move the earthlings away from peace? If the answer is "yes," then we are embarked on the proper course. Let us apply this question to your strategy regarding PUP and its plans for Peace Dove Day.

Think, dear Pharnum, how the participants in this event will feel if it is hailed universally as a success. (And by "success" will be meant, simply, that it actually came off and got lots of media coverage.) Those who took part in it will feel noble. Watch for the quotes in their papers and on television. They will say things like, "It really feels good to actually do something for world peace instead of just talking about it"; and "It was great to see so many people getting out there and making a difference." What they won't see is that they haven't actually *done* anything, that the phrase "making a difference" is meaningless. But that is their problem, not ours. We want them to think they have now "done their bit" for peace and can get back to whatever they were doing previously: being contentious, manipulative, and devious in their personal lives, for instance. When they are asked to make financial contributions to PUP or another peace organization or to do some writing of letters or phone calling or

praying for peace, they will be a bit irked. They will
feel they have done enough and will begin to wonder if
they are now going to be constantly plagued by all
kinds of "do gooder" organizations.

Consider another benefit to us which a "successful" Peace Dove Day will offer: jealousy. In fact,
just the anticipation of its success has aroused envy on
the part of other peace organizations. Their leaders are
grumbling that PUP is engaging in a "cheap publicity
stunt" to bring in funds. I view this as the seeds of
what may well become a full-grown feud within the
peace movement. Some peace groups are lending only
token support to Peace Dove Day; others are not par-
ticipating at all. What we have here is one of those
delectable ironies that we strive so hard to achieve: the
more successful Peace Dove Day appears to the
public — and the more credit PUP takes for its
success — the deeper will be the divisions among
peace activists.

So you see, Groacher, your plan to "sow discord
in the form of envy, mistrust, and power struggles" is
not at fault. But rather than working to this end within
the ranks of PUP itself, we want to create conflict
within the larger peace movement. At present, we can
best achieve that goal by insuring that PUP remains
well-organized and that Peace Dove Day is a success.

Let me comment briefly on the second aspect of
your strategy. Apparently, my old instructor Pugny Pandybat continues his excellent job of teaching B.T.S.
students the art of behavior analysis. I was one of the
first to take his now-renowned Diagnostics course. His
influence on you is apparent in your firm grasp of data
examination. Be warned, however, that Pandybat's
"conversion" to the new ideology, while necessary to
save his position, was one of form more than substance.
That is, his understanding of what makes *individuals*

tick is far more accurate than his understanding of how *groups* function. And so, while you are right that some of the PUP leaders are "single-minded" and "zealous," you err in assuming that all of them are true believers in the cause for world peace.

Some, in fact, are active in the organization because they believe PUP provides them a concrete way to put their Christian faith into action. Their primary commitment is not to PUP or its aims, but rather to the execrable One they call the Prince of Peace. They keep their critical faculties well-honed and will not hesitate to speak out against what they regard as inappropriate activities. For them, peace is not so much an end to be achieved as a means to the end of what they understand to be the Adversary's will. "We must live now as if the reign of God is present in all its fullness" is one of the statements they are fond of making. *These people are the dangerous ones.* You must distinguish them from those who think that eliminating the threat of nuclear war is the answer to the problems of humankind.

You plan to "undermine the strong convictions PUP members have about the truth of their political and moral positions." No, no, no, dear Pharnum. You must do the very opposite. Make them more zealous for *their* cause, not less. And when I say "*their* cause," I do mean for the emphasis to be on the word "their." We want them never to doubt the righteousness of their own position and, at the same time, never to doubt the unrighteousness of those who oppose them. Above all, we must keep from their consciousness the truth that they are as weak, error-prone, and just plain sinful as anyone else and that the Adversary loves them anyway. You must *not* "introduce the possibility that their chosen course just might be wrong." You must aim at making as many of them as possible convinced that the way to peace espoused by PUP is the only way.

You can see, therefore, that your approach to George Wright will have to be revised. Far from helping him to question his convictions, you must work toward reinforcing his original point of view, that in PUP he has found his *raison d'être*. And for Hades' sake, keep him away from "Hegel, Kierkegaard, and Tillich." It's true that we sometimes have used their writings to our advantage, but in George Wright's case, they will not help us. Among other things, he will be reminded that no human cause deserves "ultimate concern." If we aren't careful, he will begin to see that he has substituted a devotion to PUP for religious faith. I'm sure you recognize that idolatry continues to be one of the best weapons in our arsenal. The trick is to keep this old dodge well camouflaged.

The other truth we want to keep hidden is that peace (not merely the absence of war, but the presence of harmony, prosperity, and universal well-being all summed up in that vile Hebrew word "shalom") can never be accomplished simply by human effort. *We* know only too well — and curse the fact constantly — that this kind of peace is the Adversary's gift to the earthlings. It's up to them to acknowledge it, live by it, and invite others to do the same. Yes, of course, they pray for it all the time: "thy kingdom come, thy will be done." But rarely do they give a thought to the meaning of those words, Satan be praised. Thanks to our unrelenting efforts, many with the greatest potential for doing damage to our cause have been seduced into supposing they can create peace in the world on their own. *It is up to you to keep the PUP earthlings firmly entrenched in this errant belief.*

Now you can understand why your job, far from destroying People United for Peace, is to help it grow and succeed. Not ultimately, of course. But we have no need to worry about its ultimate success. The seeds of its own failure were planted in its philosophical origins. Its very successes will, ironically, be the cause of its eventual demise. Attention from the media will provoke attacks from rival groups. Jealousy among leaders within the PUP organization, such as that which has begun to surface between George Wright and Alice Chambers, will occur as a matter of course. Virulent criticism from right wing organizations will eventually create a persecution mentality among the PUP faithful, leading them to become more zealous, more self-righteous, and consequently less capable of recognizing the revolting truth of Francis of Assisi's prayer: that the best earthlings can hope for is to become "instruments" of the Adversary's peace.

With the greatest confidence in your ability to make the necessary revisions to your undertaking and with warmest regards, dear Pharnum, I remain,

Verruca Smutch

P.S.   A final suggestion: whenever possible, discourage the existence of a sense of humor among PUP staff and volunteers. The only kind of laughter worth anything to us is sardonic, bitter laughter made at the expense of others. A sense of humor about their own opinions and behavior can be absolutely fatal to our purposes. Keep them earnest and keep them proud of their earnestness.

*One of the exasperating problems in studying the contents of the
Groacher file is the inexplicable absence of certain documents. For
example, my best efforts failed to locate Groacher's reply to Smutch's
lengthy letter. That he made such a reply is obvious from the
peremptory contents of the following note. That he made the
mistake of taking his supervisor's "my dear Pharnum's" at face value
is also obvious.*

From the Desk of Verruca

Groacher:

You have presumed. I will not tolerate it.

First, no subordinate — I repeat, *no subordinate* —
will take the liberty of addressing me by my first name.
Such undue familiarity will not be tolerated.

Second, the instructions I made in my dispatch
are exactly that — instructions. They are meant to
carried out *to the letter*! They are not to be regarded as
"suggestions."

Third, I had no intention, nor will it ever be my
intention, of "engaging in open and honest dialogue
about strategy" with the agents under my supervision.
If I ever want your miserable opinion (and I cannot
conceive of such a circumstance), I will ask for it.
Until then, keep your "alternative proposals" to
yourself.

Fourth, and finally, any future communications
with your colleagues assigned to other peace groups
will be cleared through me first. I am not interested in
the "sampling of options" that you had the temerity
not only to solicit from your peers but also to put forth
in support of your stupid ideas. Do you think I care a
fig about the opinions of agents Epizoot and Maggunk?
(Appropriate measures have been taken to deal with

their perfidious behavior, I assure you.) Do you
suppose I run my department by majority vote?

Your future performance will be scrutinized
carefully. For your sake, it had better far surpass what
has preceded it.

Emphatically yours,

Supervisor Smutch

8.

Groacher And
HARVEST

What transpired with Groacher at this point must remain in the realm of supposition. The only clue as to what really happened comes from the next note addressed to him by his one friend, Gordo Glummer. I use the word friend advisedly, of course. Strictly speaking, friendship as such does not exist among demons. The closest thing to it is a kind of "misery loves company" phenomenon. From what can be learned about the relationship between Glummer and Groacher, it seems to have originated in the Bureau of Diabolic Records to which Groacher was once demoted and where Glummer continues to labor. Apparently, Groacher found in Gordo Glummer a demon with whom he could commiserate.

Although no human friendship is entirely free of self-interest (such friendships often founder, in fact, when one or both of the persons involved can no longer find a satisfactory answer to the question, "What am I getting out of this relationship?"), personal advantage is evidently the only rationale demons have for relationships. It is obvious that Groacher uses Glummer as a sounding board. His letters to Glummer frequently include boasts about his own accomplishments and complaints about working conditions, colleagues, and supervisors. Groacher also uses Glummer's access to statistics to his advantage.

It is harder to say what Glummer gets out of the relationship. Limited as he is to his low-level position in the Records Bureau, he perhaps uses Groacher to experience vicariously the adventures of field assignments. Glummer also has an insatiable craving for gossip of every kind. The letter which follows alludes to this need. His mild berating of Groacher for not including more "stuff you found out about our classmate Putridemus" can be understood in this regard.

To: Pharnum

From: Gordo

Re: The latest scuttlebutt

Dear Pharnum,

Long time no hear from. Yes, you have dropped me a few brief notes occasionally. But you know what I mean. You haven't written anything of *substance* lately. (A few sentences describing weather conditions in Oregon hardly qualifies as substantive!)

You know how important it is for me to get a feel for life out there on the front lines. I want to know the scoop on your new boss Squnt. Don't tell me he's "much like all the others" you've dealt with. Details — I want details! Have you fallen afoul of that hair-trigger temper Squnt reputedly has? Are his office walls really decorated with photographs of all the earthling celebrities whose downfall he claims to have had a hand in causing? I've heard Squnt likes to regale his agents with war stories about his successes and presses on them autographed copies of his book, *Some Big Ones That Didn't Get Away: My Personal Success Gallery from Nero to Nixon*. If he hasn't given you a copy yet, it's probably because the liberals' denunciation of the "cult of personality" school has made him more cautious about such displays.

I'm also eager to hear more about some of the field agents you mentioned in your last note. How in Satan's name did Lepsy Toxinson manage to suck in with know-it-all Verruca Smutch? He always struck me as having the political savvy of a jackass. And what about the rumor which claims that Borry Grassgrovel has been sentenced to a term at the Reorientation Center because she was caught in "treasonable acts of sympathy" with a group of earthling refugees she was assigned to? Really, Pharnum, the stuff you found out about our old classmate Putridemus was much too tame for me. So he's "under surveillance by the Field Agent Police." Big deal. Isn't everyone?

I can understand why you have been feeling down lately. If only you had known ahead of time Smutch was so touchy, you might have been able to keep yourself out of trouble. I realize getting canned from the Self-Interest Group Division doesn't look good on your résumé, but it was better for you to get reassigned than to hang on where Smutch could vent her rage at you.

It's time to look ahead. What possibilities for advancement do you have there in the Anti-Religious Growth Bureau? There is no pretending this is anything but a demotion for you. Our overall secularism strategy has paid off so well that "religious growth" is not causing much concern these days. Still, there are opportunities for achievement. Maybe you will get assigned to Africa where Christianity continues to spread rapidly. Let's hope you don't get another U.S.A. assignment where Christianity has been on the wane for a long time.

Anyway, let me hear from you. If you come through with some juicy tidbits, in my next letter I'll give you some really hot news about the infighting in the Freedom Party.

Cordially,

Gordo

Of only passing interest is Groacher's brief reply to Glummer in which he half-heartedly tries to accede to his friend's request for "juicy tidbits." However, Groacher does mention that his placement within the Anti-Religious Growth Bureau is more favorable than he had hoped for. Assigned to an ecumenical organization called HARVEST, Groacher has specific responsibility for subverting their publication program. He explains to Glummer that HARVEST is a cooperative venture among mainline Protestant churches in the United States and Canada which have suffered membership decline. By working together, they can keep costs down and, as Groacher puts it, "keep alive the illusion that they are more concerned about the church of J – – – – C – – – – – than they are about their own denominations."

What follows are the notes from which Groacher drafted his report to his superior, D.T. Squnt. (Unfortunately the report itself could not be accessed.) I have extracted from Groacher's notes his comments relative to the publication of a new manual designed to help churches attract new members.

NOTES

1) Re: Publication Team

Team headed by George Smiley who appears to be making a concerted effort to live up to his name. Smiles all the time and is always jovial with other team members and support staff ("How's it goin' today, Jack?" and lots of hearty slaps on the back). This behavior probably a coverup for his insecurity about his new job. Comes from a poor Southern family, got an athletic scholarship at a liberal arts college in Iowa, and left behind his fundamentalist upbringing. Rose quickly in the ranks of his church and now has the panicky feeling he is in over his head.

Smiley's closest competition for the post of Publications Executive = Jack Wells, the most outspoken member of the Publication Team. By nature, a malcontent. Resents Smiley and will drop comments around colleagues such as: "Well, George is *Lutheran*, after all. Have you ever seen a Lutheran who knew anything about evangelism?" A Canadian, Wells misses no chance to show contempt for what he calls "the Uncle Sam mentality."

Only other team member with clout = Mildred Sumner. Best thinker in the group, works behind the scenes to exert her influence, wins her points by being sweetly reasonable. Potentially dangerous.

Team is working under a deadline; new manual publication date is 10 months away. Smiley's big problem = trying to get cooperation out of a team of staff members with differing ideas on what should be included in the manual.

APPROACH

- Work for maximum discord among team members.
- Play on Jack Wells' jealousy of Smiley and Well's anti-American bias.
- Keep Smiley privately anticipating conflict; his apprehension will fuel the fire.
- Block from Smiley's mind the possibility of publicly acknowledging the conflicts and dealing with them openly.
- Encourage him to keep up the charade that "everything is dandy."
- Have him keep reminding himself that, after all, Christians love each other.

- See to it that he makes the old mistake of
  supposing that "loving" means the same thing as
  "liking."
- Make sure he continues his practice of telling
  visitors "we're all one big happy family here in
  Publications." Eventually, he will believe this lie
  himself and be even less likely to bring about
  honest expression of feelings.
- Remember the old Hadesian axiom: "one buried
  resentment is worth a handful of quarrels."

2) Re: Title of Manual

As expected, choosing a title for manual =
excellent forum for airing conflicting opinions and
personal grievances. In an effort to foster the illusion
of a democratic process for team decisions, Smiley
proposed title for the manual and then, in a staff
meeting, invited discussion. Wanted the final decision made, as he put it, "on a consensus basis." His
proposed title, *The Vineyard Conspiracy*, had a few
supporters, but they went along with it mostly
because they knew it was Smiley's idea.

Smiley's reasons for his choice:

- It's biblical. Lots of vine/vineyard/grapes/wine
  imagery in the Bible; "conspiracy" suggests Jesus'
  advice to disciples to be "wise as serpents, innocent as doves."
- It fits with name of the organization, HARVEST.
  "Fields white onto harvest," HARVEST's
  text/slogan, elicits agrarian, pastoral imagery;
  "vineyard" is in keeping with this approach.
- It's "sexy." From purely marketing approach, the
  word "conspiracy" in title has appeal; makes
  book sound more like a spy novel than a book
  about church growth.

Opposition to Smiley's title proposal led by Wells. Attacked it on grounds of unsound strategy in using rural imagery (vineyards) to appeal to modern readers: "Are we trying to sell this book to a bunch of farmers?" Also disputed Smiley's claim that putting vineyard and conspiracy together in the title would work. As he put it, "sexy is one thing, stupid is another!"

Sumner raised the issue of honesty. Quietly suggested that "perhaps we had better give some thought to whether or not we want our title to mislead our readers. It may be better to be descriptive of the book's contents than to promise something the book cannot deliver."

Result = no consensus reached. Smiley good-naturedly thanked the dissenters for their "constructive criticism" and set another meeting time "so we can all give this some thought and prayer."

APPROACH

– Keep the dispute over the title simmering. This conflict has a chance to become symbolic of the deeper dissension that exists. Probably better to push for Smiley to get his way on the title so resentment against him can build.
– Encourage a confederacy between Wells and Sumner on this issue.
– Work to create other conflicts between Wells and Sumner to ensure continuing turmoil on the team.

3) **Re: Controversy Over Manual's Contents**

Unexpected division emerging in the ranks of the publication team. Personal enmity between Smiley and Wells as sharp as ever (luckily). Oddly enough, they share similar convictions about what should be in the manual re: how to encourage growth in church membership. Sumner female represents a minority viewpoint in several ways, but her low-key approach has won her a hearing among team members.

All on the team agree that increasing the number of church members is desirable. Some feel church's influence in society is at stake, if not its very survival. Especially frustrating to them is the numerical growth of independent, pentecostal, and sectarian groups, as well as those churches sometimes lumped into the "evangelical" category. But while members of the publication team agree that membership growth is important, they differ on what strategies to use and therefore what the manual should contain.

Wells favors a "needs analysis" approach. One of his favorite statements = "We must ask what people are looking for in a church and then respond to that." (Note his background in market research.) Carries in his briefcase at all times numerous charts and statistics relating to North American churchgoers' income, level of education, attitudes on social issues, etc. Uses such data to support his contention that "people today want to believe, they want bedrock certainty, they want to make confident moral choices." Points to the fastest growing churches in the U.S.A. and Canada as those which offer such "certainty" to their members.

Smiley also favors a pragmatic approach. His constant question = "What works?" Gets impatient with Wells for frequently quoting statistics, but is impressed by what Wells calls "the hard core evidence" about growing churches. Smiley favors producing a manual that will appeal to people's fascination for bigness. Argues that by making people feel they can be part of a large, influential group, a church can draw to itself many who feel insignificant in their jobs and their place in the community. Points to the success of the best-known television churches as an example of this phenomenon. Has written the lead sentence to the first chapter: "The bottom line in effective evangelism is whether the church grows: a church that isn't adding to its numbers is a dying church."

Sumner has increasingly been resisting this kind of thinking. Criticized a rough draft of Jack Wells' "list of needs" which he submitted for inclusion in the manual. List included needs that were personal (coping with stress, how to stop smoking); spiritual (how to study the Bible, learning to pray); marital (communicating with your spouse, dealing with children on drugs); and relational (learning to listen, how to deepen your friendships). Sumner acknowledged these as bona fide human needs but lamented the absence of any category reflecting "the need to use one's abilities for productive endeavors." Said Sumner, "A church that does nothing but appeal to the 'what's in it for me' attitude has betrayed its calling." Her thoughtful manner and even-tempered disposition have begun to influence several members of the publication team.

APPROACH

- Bring this burgeoning conflict of ideas to a head as soon as possible.
- Help Sumner gain enough additional support to make the controversy a standoff.
- With these methodological differences added to the personality clash between Wells and Smiley, there is an excellent chance that the publication deadline will not be met. As it nears, pressure on the entire team will mount. With luck, the whole enterprise could collapse. Even if it doesn't, the clash of opinions will certainly become public and could well spread to the upper ranks of the HARVEST organization. Work to this end.

Groacher's detailed report apparently prompted his boss Squnt to submit a progress report to his superior Cozenby Trumper. In response, Trumper discussed Groacher's performance in a lengthy memo reviewing the work of several demonic agents assigned to HARVEST.

To: D. T. Squnt, Secondary Operative
Church Bureaucracy Division
Heretic Square
Hades

From: Cozenby Trumper
Executive for Baneful Despoliation
Mephistopheles Court
Hades

Re: Your report on Groacher's progress

As to the work of agent Groacher, I am generally in agreement with your assessment. He has made a mess of things. Where in Hell did you find this numbskull? For your sake, Squnt, I hope he wasn't your personal choice for the publication team assignment. If so, you can expect a very poor mark in the personnel management category on your next performance rating. But maybe you got stuck with him because someone pulled some strings on his behalf. . .or more likely, dumped him on you to get you into trouble. If so, I'll try to show some leniency.

Like you, I find it hard to believe that Groacher would actually suppose that his mission was to *prevent* publication of *The Vineyard Conspiracy*. I know you believe in giving your agents lots of free rein in their work, but I really am surprised that you would allow him to make such a major blunder. It will be up to you to take appropriate measures for salvaging the situation. Perhaps Groacher can defuse the controversy on the publication team in time to ensure publication of the manual.

You write in your report: "While we all have grave concern about the potential membership growth in churches, there is one thing that concerns us even more — the growth in spiritual maturity, genuine faith, and committed discipleship among the earthlings who have fallen under the spell of the Other Side."

Exactly, Squnt, exactly! That is why we have such a vested interest in seeing to it that churches concentrate more on numerical growth than on growth of any other kind. How the earthlings can be so stupid about their conviction that growth is always desirable is beyond me. Cancer grows (Satan be praised!), but that is hardly the kind of growth earthlings find beneficial. It is to our advantage to keep them foolishly pursuing growth in numbers at any cost.

I find it amusing that those who spend time concocting schemes for adding names to the church roll will frequently point to the record of the early church in spreading rapidly from a handful of believers to encompass the Roman Empire. What they miss is the fact that this growth was not accomplished by any grand strategy for bringing in large numbers of people. Growth in the early days just happened as the followers of J – – – – lived out their faith. Hell suffered many painful defeats until a suitable counter strategy was developed. Fortunately for us, we have now honed that strategy to near razor edge.

Which brings me back to the situation that Groacher has been dealing with. Every member of the publication committee (with one apparent exception) is firmly convinced that church membership is always a good thing. Luckily for us, they subscribe to the "bigger is better" theory. This means we can concentrate on our perennially successful program of using a desirable end to justify any means whatsoever. The best example is our old friend Charlemagne who had his soldiers line up the captured "heathen" and give them a choice of being baptized or slaughtered. Such methods are too heavy-handed these days, but the principle still applies: make the appeal to becoming a member of the church so far removed from genuine conversion that there will be almost nothing "Christian" about it.

In fact, a good bit of this principle is already at work. Surveys of American and Canadian church people indicate that the more seriously they take church membership, the more racist and chauvinistic they are, the less capable of loving their enemies. This is precisely the kind of thing we need to encourage. What a coup for our Cause: by helping churches grow, we end up with more people than before who have the very attitudes we promote! Of all my accomplishments, Squnt, I am most proud of this one.

On the other hand, there is something to be said for the very opposite approach, the tried and true method of encouraging people *not* to take their church membership seriously. The point here is to make them feel that having their names on a church roll means they have taken care of their religious needs. We know from experience with millions of these pitiful creatures that membership in a church can be an alternative to authentic commitment and can stand in the way of true faith.

Yet perhaps our biggest dilemma comes in dealing with the many people who stay away from any church involvement on the basis of their distrust of "organized religion." At first thought, it would seem logical for us to leave well enough alone. That is the policy I have always followed. Lately though, I am beginning to wonder if we aren't missing a golden opportunity here. Many of these earthlings are honest, caring people with real concern about any number of the very plagues we take such enjoyment in promoting: poverty, discrimination, destruction of the environment, etc.

Wouldn't it be better for us in the long run to work toward getting these people into church? I'm merely asking a rhetorical question, Squnt. There is danger, of course, the danger that always besets us when we are dealing with the church. For all its stupidities and failures, it is still the one institution that has the potential for destroying all the gains we have made. For reasons we cannot decipher, the Adversary has seen fit to entrust the church with spiritual resources that make me tremble even to think about. Those who take the step of committing themselves to a church and make even the scantest efforts to participate

in its life have the potential for receiving what the
Adversary has chosen to call "abundant life." Hearing
an occasional sermon, dull as it may be, can have surprisingly life-changing effects. Partaking of that singu-
larly pernicious meal of bread and wine may touch the
life of the most apathetic of believers.

Particularly harmful, from our standpoint, is the
influence that a loving community of these Christians
can have on souls that we have firmly in our grasp.
How maddeningly true it is that love in the church can
cover a multitude of sins. The music in worship may
be execrable, the theology full of holes, the church
program an organizational shambles...and we do our
best to promote these conditions...but we are almost
helpless against the power of the Adversary's ultimate
weapon: the simple love of one person for another. The
church, for all its weaknesses, has love going for it.
That fact puts our policy of encouraging numerical
growth as a means of weakening the Christian cause
very much at risk. Still, history bears out the irony so
dear to our hearts: that any religion which grows large
enough to dominate the society in which it finds itself
will perpetrate wonderfully rich varieties of injustice
on that society. It is to our credit that we have been
able to subvert so much of what the church *might* have
accomplished.

So, again, I ask if it might be better for us to
lure into the church some of the very people who have
been resisting it. By redirecting their dangerous concerns for the betterment of society to harmless matters
such as whether or not to expand the church parking
lot or disputes about what color to paint the church
office, we can disarm a potentially damaging group.
This technique, formally designated as "P-13" in the
old training manuals, is better known by its popular
name, "the vaccination strategy." It consists, as you

doubtless recall, of taking people, however motivated they may be to become Christians, and inoculating them against Christianity. That is, by giving them a weakened or twisted form of the gospel, we can keep them from ever "catching" the real thing.

Yet I fear that such a bright bunch as the publication committee might not fall for the old dodges. If they see past the usual seductions we use on new church members, they could begin a movement within the church establishment to begin taking the gospel seriously. Needless to say, Squnt, I don't wish to be the one who would have such a debacle laid at my doorstep! However, I would be happy to hear your views on this matter. If we ever deploy such a strategy, we will need a united front.

For the time being, let us concentrate on undermining the influence of Mildred Sumner on the publication team. She has been getting uncomfortably close to seeing through our smokescreen. For example, she keeps talking about "the way of the cross." So long as no one sees the implication of that kind of language for the church, all is well. But we simply cannot have her ideas influence decision making in regard to what actually will appear in the manual. We have done an excellent job in getting the humans to believe "it is only natural" for the church to want to grow. They keep telling themselves that the larger and more powerful the church is, the more it can accomplish. That is true enough, of course, in earthly terms. And it is precisely "in earthly terms" that we want them to think.

The accepted standard in what Europeans and North Americans vainly call "Western civilization" has become the "can do" attitude. It is a viewpoint which allows only for success, which will not admit even the possibility of failure. Growth, advancement, and progress are the bywords. Never mind that if the rate of consumption of the West were extended to the rest of the globe, the earth's resources would be depleted in short order. To acknowledge and act on that fact would be to engage in negative thinking, the one thing not permitted. The modern credo is, "We can master anything we set our wills to master."

You can see what a great job we have done in getting the North American churches to buy into the "can do" point of view. What has prompted the mainline churches to pool their resources in the HARVEST venture is not so much their longing to be faithful to the gospel as their worry that diminishing numbers in their ranks gives the appearance of failure. What a shrewdly diabolical accomplishment on our part it has been to convince them — and nearly everyone else — that appearance is more important than substance, that *appearance is everything!*

Now you can see why we must somehow destroy the growing influence of Mildred Sumner on the publication team. She understands that what the Adversary desires the church to be is not a "success" in terms of size, influence, and status, but rather a grain of salt, a bit of yeast in society.

Another serious problem with Sumner is that, unlike other team members, she has spotted our hand. She recognizes that the great concern for growth among church leaders is a direct result of our efforts. Most of her colleagues pride themselves as being too liberal, too "enlightened," to acknowledge our existence. As you know, our best ploy has been to convince intellectuals that belief in our Malevolent Lord is a vestige of outmoded theology.

(I find it interesting, by the way, that earthlings have debated the assertion of Nietzsche: "without God everything is permitted." But, so far, they have not

recognized that they have swallowed whole the converse of Nietzsche's idea, which is that "without the
Devil everything is possible." It is imperative that we
keep them under the spell of this illusion.)

Yes, it's true that a few voices like Jacques
Ellul's and the Canadian theologian Douglas John
Hall's have been raised in protest against the prevailing
view. Hall, for instance, has lamented that, "The sense
of the demonic has gone out of contemporary church
Christianity."* Fortunately, we have been able to keep
that kind of thinking from attracting much attention
among church policy makers.

It is obvious that Mildred Sumner *has* been
influenced by such ideas. Her remarkable understanding of the Adversary's methods and her insights into
the situation she faces on her job cause me grave
concern. She has been saying things like, "How can
the church be faithful to the Crucified One if we
measure our faithfulness by the success standards of
the world?" And, "Instead of using market analysis to
help us decide what the church should be, ought we
not to be asking what Christ is calling us to become?" I
don't need to remind you, Squnt, of the alarming danger such statements represent.

Let me strongly recommend that you counter-
attack. Instruct Groacher (or better still, his replacement)
to convince Smiley and Wells that they should lay
aside their personal grievances in order to present a
united front against Sumner's powerful critique. One of
the advantages we have over the forces of Heaven will
be of help here. The more humans come under the

---

*ED. NOTE: from Lighten Our Darkness *by Douglas John Hall.*

influence of the Other Side, the more trusting they
grow, the more likely to "become as little children."
It's hard to believe that the Adversary really desires this
condition in them, but we have it on record that child-
like trust is not only a desirable trait from Heaven's
point of view, but also a precondition for entering the
"kingdom."

We learned long ago that temptation is most successful (and most satisfying to us!) the closer these
poor mortals get to Heaven's gate. Thus, we can use the
graciousness of the Sumner creature against her. She
knows that Wells and Smiley hold opposing views, but
she is unwilling to impute evil to their motives. She
tells herself that "after all, their intentions are good."
She is wrong, of course, but that is beside the point.
As a Christian who has steadily progressed in her
odious goal of "having the mind of Christ," Sumner
realizes she should give others the benefit of the doubt.
This makes her personality winsome, naturally, and is
one of the contrivances the Adversary uses to attract
earthlings to her. As a result, they soon learn about the
resources of faith she draws on. But her unwillingness
to be judgmental also makes her vulnerable to our
tactics. She is neither stupid nor weak (more's the
pity), but she does have chinks in her armor.

Both Smiley and Wells are beginning to fancy
that Sumner's opposing views are personal attacks
directed at them. Those who come under our influence, you see, are never charitable as to the motives of
people they judge to be their enemies. We teach them
to become expert in the use of suspicion and cynicism.
It will take but a whisper to convince these two
creatures that Sumner is aiming at seizing the executive
position held by Smiley and coveted by Wells. Each
will find it to his political advantage to make common
cause to ward off this imagined threat. As I see it, a

forceful denunciation of Sumner's views in the next
staff meeting would make an excellent maneuver. Taken
completely by surprise, she will likely be devastated.
Whether she retorts angrily to their accusations (not
likely given her personality) or withdraws into injured
silence, the damage will have been done. Her fledgling
supporters will melt away.

Have Smiley and Wells use the old sectarian
argument. They can accuse Sumner of advocating an
untenable purist position (throwing in the word
"puritan" and its derivatives is always a good ruse if it
is handled carefully). They can accuse her of wanting
to keep the church from "muddying her skirts" (a nice
sexist touch), but that this would be a step back "to the
dark ages." Let them characterize Sumner's views as
"the course of cowardice, a failure of nerve, a blueprint
for disaster." (Please remember that I was a speechwriter
in the old days, Squnt; I can't resist turning a phrase
now and then!)

Above all, have them point out that Sumner's
position is rooted in a perverse sort of pride. Have
them argue that, by resisting growth in numbers, by
criticizing the drive to be successful, she is consigning
the church to the sin of false martyrdom; she is push-
ing the church to glory in its littleness or poverty or
lack of worldly prestige; she is asking the church to
equate being misunderstood with faithfulness to Christ.
There is enough truth to this argument — and Sumner
is astute enough to recognize it — that it will doubtless
be the *coup de grâce.* I'm sure you remember enough
from your courses in logic and debate to persuade
Wells and Smiley to save this thrust for their closing
remarks.

As for Pharnum Groacher. . .well, I'm afraid he
really must go. I agree that he does have a certain innocent charm about him. His intentions are so very noble!

But, as the earthlings put it, "the road to Hell is paved with good intentions." They often use this expression as a kind of rueful commentary about someone who tries hard and fails. On the other hand, they may employ the phrase to issue a damning indictment of someone who holds an opposing view. Conservatives use it to put down "bleeding heart liberals," liberals to score against "knee jerk reactionaries," etc. What they usually do not realize is that the Adversary actually does put some stock in good intentions. This is a mystery to us (a particularly repugnant one, I might add). Luckily for our Cause, good intentions alone will not suffice to save the necks of the earthlings — even the Adversary isn't that crazy!

We, of course, cannot afford to be even remotely sentimental about such things. Groacher has botched it; *ipso facto*, he must pay the price. Let me confide in you about a further suspicion I have. I have not met this agent personally. You have and can therefore judge. Have you detected even the faintest odor of. . .I hesitate to use the word. . .*goodness* on him? There are rare cases where the necessary associations our agents must make with the humans may result in infestations of *goodness*. And Groacher has spent a great deal of his efforts dealing with the wretched Sumner creature.

I know, Squnt, I know. Official orthodoxy in Hell does not even admit this possibility. (The same is true, by the way, of most Christian orthodoxy; we have at least some things in common!) Nevertheless, I have heard stories. . .

It would be wise to keep this last just between us. I am probably letting my suspicions get out of hand, even for a Fifth Rank devil, ha ha. And I have no *proof* that the influence of the Other Side extends to our realm. Nevertheless, it seems to me we err whenever we do not take very seriously the Molten Rule of

Hell: "Never underestimate the power of the Adversary." Therefore — and this is a direct order, not a suggestion — in your final meeting with Groacher, you will take deep sniffs. You will do this so covertly that Groacher will not be able to testify against you if subpoenaed by the Heresy Tribunal. If you catch even a *trace* of the abominable stench on him that I suspect is there, report it to me at once. I give you my personal assurance that a failure to carry out this order will have dire consequences for you.

You may tell Groacher that he is being relieved of his assignment at once. I will handle the bureaucratic mess that transfers always entail.

Emphatically,

Cozenby Trumper
Executive for Baneful Despoliation,
Fifth Rank, Second Class

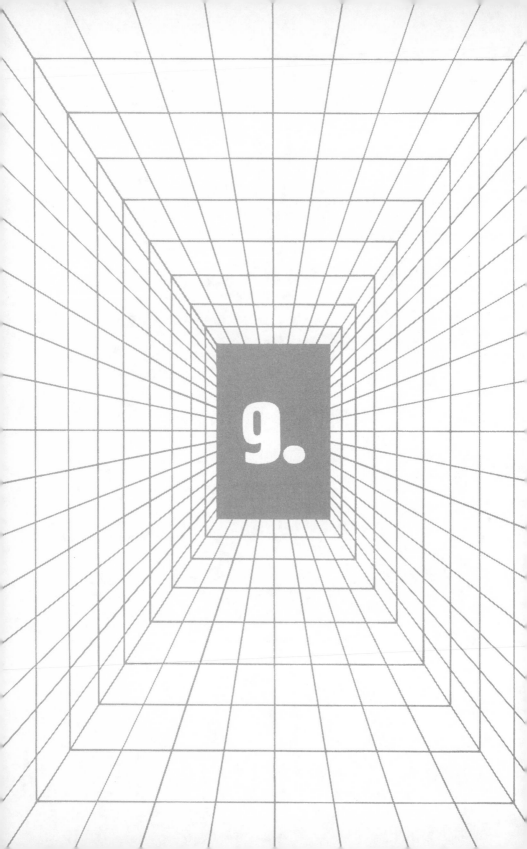

9.

Groacher Returns To Grovedale

"What has been is what will be," murmured Koheleth, "and what has been done will be done; and there is nothing new under the sun" (Ecclesiates 1:9).

It may be a misuse of Scripture to apply it to the fate of demons, but these words do have particular relevance to the next turn in Pharnum Groacher's exceptionally sinuous career.

Once again there is no record of what lay behind the decision relative to Groacher's next, and somewhat surprising, assignment: a return to the Grovedale Church. Groacher's own word to Glummer testifies that reassignments to previous posts are not all that uncommon in Hell, especially when performance of the agent in question has been found wanting. Apparently being reassigned is a way of symbolizing an agent's "fall from grace," though a more inappropriate metaphor for what transpires in the Hadesian realm is hard to imagine!

Whatever the reasons for it, the reappointment of Groacher to Grovedale produced unexpected results. Within a relatively short time, evaluations of Groacher's efforts by his superiors were most favorable. Some reports of his work might even be described as glowing. Unlike several of the earlier episodes documented in the Groacher file, details of the second Grovedale assignment are confirmed by extensive data. Letters, reports, memos, and other materials abound.

Among the reams of available material, I have selected two documents. The first is a sample of the by-now-familiar correspondence between Groacher and Gordo Glummer. It is of special interest because it comes fairly early in Groacher's tenure (again, the absence of accurate dating is a nightmare). Unlike Groacher's reports to his superiors, which are too blatantly self-serving to be trusted for accuracy, his letters to Glummer can be relied on to paint a reasonably accurate picture about the situation in the Grovedale Church and Groacher's feelings about his work.

The second document I've selected is quite unusual. Its very existence reflects the positive recognition Groacher attained for his achievements during his second stint at the Grovedale Church. More about this document later.

To: Gordo

From: Pharnum

Re: My reassignment

Dear Gordo,

I'm sure you have heard the news by now...I'm back here at Grovedale. As you might expect, my first reaction to being reassigned was anything but positive. We've all heard stories of field agents being sent back to posts they had previously held. These reassignments are never publicized officially, of course, but the word gets around. I remember your telling me that Gimcrack, who graduated in the class after us, had messed up a big opportunity at AT&T (it was a junior position, but still quite a step up for her) and been sent back to her original assignment, a Rotary Club in Cedar Rapids, Iowa.

When I learned I was headed back to Grovedale, I tried to console myself that at least they had spared me the ignominy of that little town in Vermont. Remember Needmore? Looking back on it now, I can laugh at the way I screwed up that situation. I do wonder how that poor old soul Pastor Trimble is getting on these days. Did he ever recover from that "Sharing God's Talents" fiasco? The only positive things that came of my time at Needmore were 1) I did learn a few things, and 2) I was assigned to the Records Bureau where you and I got acquainted.

I know you enjoy hearing the latest dirt, Gordo, but I don't have much to pass on this time. Have you heard the latest about Synica Snidemuller, that old biddy who tried to do me in when I worked with the Warren Foundation? It turns out she has gotten herself into very deep muck. She evidently has been found guilty of conspiring with Malchus Gnashwell (remember how he got demoted for encouraging a "personal sin" policy?) and some other top level people in the conservative underground.

Surprised I knew about this? Well, while I was working on the HARVEST project I picked up some rumors from some of my fellow agents. With your interest in political intrigue (personally, I find such stuff as dull as petty theft), I knew you would enjoy hearing some scuttlebutt. The scoop on Snidemuller is by far the most interesting thing I've heard. Let me know if you learn what has become of her. I'd also like to know who was given her position as Supervisor of Agents Assigned to Foundations. That's a spot I would love to occupy myself someday, Lucifer willing.

But for now, I have my hands full here at Grovedale. I must admit it was fascinating to see how things have developed during my absence. Looking back on how green I was when I came here right out of training school, I'm amazed at how well I did, really. True, I was done in by that PIA ruse of falsifying correspondence from Heaven (the most embarrassing episode of my career). But up to that point, I had accomplished quite a bit with this church. By comparison, my successor Spalpeen was simply not up to the job.

Not only did the church add a significant number of people to its membership during Spalpeen's time, but the types of people added are noteworthy. They are mostly a young, energetic bunch with an interest in spiritual growth — in short, the most dangerous kind of Christians. (Luckily, this means they also have the greatest potential for evil if I can manage to win them over to our side.)

The pastoral team at Grovedale is one of my major obstacles. All three of them — two males and a female — have an unfortunate combination of talent, commitment, and solid faith. Their style of leadership, which creatively combines challenge and kindly concern for the members of the church, has helped make Grovedale a force to be reckoned with. To make matters worse, the staff works well together; they have the ability to air their differences openly in an atmosphere of mutual support. Not much room to maneuver there, I fear.

Still, I have some ideas I want to try on the Grovedale folks. I see possibilities for disrupting the positive spirit that presently exists here. Wish me luck this time around, Gordo.

Sincerely,

Pharnum

Unique among the documents in the Groacher file is an article found in Harpies' Monthly, a prestigious journal which is apparently "must" reading for all demonic agents. The issue containing the article in question is devoted to first-devil accounts of successful field work within a variety of religious organizations. Under an article entitled "The Rewards of Parish Work" appears the byline: Pharnum Groacher. This article was written at a much later point than Groacher's letter to Gordo Glummer. While Groacher cannot resist some of his old braggadocio, the accomplishments he reports

*bear unmistakable marks of authenticity. More than ever before,
he is content to let the facts speak for themselves. Also noteworthy is his firm grasp of the situation he is dealing with at Grovedale.*

I have selected pertinent excerpts from the article.

---

*The Rewards of Parish Work:
What I Found at Grovedale Church and How I Am Subverting It*

by Pharnum Groacher

After engaging in field work that has been richly varied
and uncommonly rewarding, I have been fortunate
enough, thank Satan, to achieve significant results in a
church parish setting. I am grateful to the editors of
this journal for inviting me to share my experience
with their readers.

The Grovedale Church consists of 850 members.
It boasts an annual budget of nearly $300,000. In other
words, here is an organization that has potential for
doing great damage to our Cause. But as we all know,
the converse is also true. . .here is an organization with
resources for *advancing* our Cause. Early in my assignment to Grovedale, I saw that my strategy must concentrate on two primary movements in the life of this
parish.

The first of these was the great interest, especially among a corps of committed church members, in
what they were calling "spiritual renewal." As the term
itself suggests, there had been concern that the
spiritual climate at Grovedale was at a low ebb. The
pastoral staff had observed this condition and had cam-
paigned successfully to initiate a varied program of
prayer groups, Bible studies, retreats, etc. When I
arrived on the scene, a dangerous spiritual growth
process was in full bloom. Fortunately, I did not make

the mistake less experienced demons often commit: that of trying to destroy the process. Instead, I asked myself the crucial question: how can I subvert the enthusiasm for spiritual growth into a gain for us? Some careful strategizing helped me find appropriate answers to this question.

I began by trying to understand what had brought about this spiritual renewal. It soon became evident that it was rooted in a reaction to the barrenness of the earthlings' lives. Many of them had come to church in the first place looking for something more than they found in their daily routines. They weren't sure what this "more" was, but they hoped religion would help them find it. Here, of course, is one of the oldest stratagems the Adversary has employed. By creating the humans with a need for relationship with Heaven, the Adversary always operates with the odds stacked in Heaven's favor. It was the despicable Augustine who expressed it most accurately in his oft-quoted line:

Thou hast made us for Thyself,
and our hearts are restless till they find
their rest in Thee.*

That's what we are up against, fellow demons!

Fortunately, we have been able to make the humans content with much less than the One they are seeking. The church has unwittingly been a primary means of helping us accomplish this end. The humans come seeking "more." Very well, we give them "more". . . more meetings to attend, more causes to be concerned about, more information to digest. Usually, they accept this. They tell themselves, "This is what the church offers, so it must be faith." But they avoid

*ED. NOTE: from Confessions of St. Augustine, Book 1, Chapter 1.

dealing with the deep, unconscious cry in their souls: "Then why do I still feel empty and alone?"

Most of the humans who come to Grovedale have been too well-schooled in skepticism to find authoritarian dogma an option. When it comes to faith, they are unwilling to disengage their brains. This causes us problems, of course (we always thrive best where humans blindly follow someone who *tells* them what to believe), but we can turn it to our advantage by making skepticism an element of faith. When the humans can be convinced that "intellectual integrity" is the keystone of their belief, we have won a major victory. The whole enterprise of the Adversary becoming "the Word made flesh" will begin to appear absurd. We must always ride hard on this apparent absurdity and keep them wondering why the great Creator of the worlds should care a hoot about the poor, pathetic earthlings and take such pains to make "abundant life" available to them. (It really *is* absurd, of course. The only ones who can accept it are those who have experienced one of the many forms of the nauseous love which has its source in Heaven.)

However, like all our strategies, the rational skepticism ploy has its own principle of diminishing returns. When it becomes too successful, as it had at Grovedale, reaction may set in. A few will allow that unconscious question, "Then why do I still feel empty and alone?" to become conscious. As I have stated, when this question emerged in the Grovedale Church, a spiritual renewal program was born.

If our own strategies have their Achilles' heels, it is a relief to know that Heaven's strategies do as well. Part of our responsibility as competent demonic agents is to be thoroughly familiar with Heaven's vulnerable places. When I first surveyed the array of spiritual weapons being brandished at Grovedale, I shuddered.

Prayer had come out of the closet*...an amazing and
frightening thing for a church that prided itself on
being "liberal." Several groups and a large number of
individuals were taking prayer seriously. Many had
begun keeping spiritual journals.

Silent retreats had enabled others to discover the
power of meditation for the first time. Even fasting had
been reborn as a vital spiritual discipline. In short, the
situation was desperate. Luckily, I remembered one of
the principles I had learned in my previous field work
assignments: if you cannot dissuade humans from a
spiritual truth, then make them fanatical about it. By
putting this principle to work, I soon made headway.

Members of the prayer groups began saying
what a shame it was that so few in the church were
"serious enough about their faith" to join a prayer
group. The ones who had found fasting a source of
strength criticized the Hunger Action Group for over-
emphasizing the physical aspects of food. Those who
had discovered in meditative silence a solid support for
their lives began muttering about how "noisy" Sunday
morning worship had become. A delightful aura of
superiority and exclusiveness emerged in the circle of
those who could (and did, whenever possible!) talk
authoritatively about the spiritual "classics." A new
"in" group had been born. Those who could discuss
the relative merits of Thomas Kelly, Evelyn Underhill,
Thomas a Kempis, and Simone Weill were "in";
everyone else was "out."

In all modesty, one of my best successes at
Grovedale was my skillful nudging of the normal
human tendency to be enthusiastic about spiritual
discovery into full-blown pride. With some practice,

---

*ED NOTE: Groacher is not a subtle demon. This pun is almost cer-
tainly inadvertent. Matthew 6:6 actually reads, in the King James
Version, "But thou, when thou prayest, enter into thy closet..."

this technique can be mastered with remarkable ease. The earthlings seem almost eager to accommodate us by falling into this trap. It is then merely a logical extension of this success to lead them into the fateful separation of the spiritual world from the material world. Once we have accomplished this, the subversion of spirituality is all but complete.

The best approach is to encourage those who have found great rewards in their spiritual growth to allow this experience to overshadow every other aspect of their lives. It is well to have them think in terms of "before" and "after"; e.g., "*before* I attended the prayer retreat, I was continually stressed out on my job, but *now* I have the spiritual resources to cope with all kinds of pressure." The trick here is to use a genuine spiritual experience to color their thinking about every aspect of their existence. We want them to get to the point where they begin thinking, and saying aloud, that nothing matters but the "life of the spirit." They will naturally find fault with church members who devote their energies to social issues and political problems.

By driving this wedge between the spiritual and the material world at Grovedale, I was able to bring about the kind of contention that most demonic agents only dream about. Both groups did much talking about "reality." But each had a different definition for that word. The spiritual growth people insisted that reality was "the interior life." The social activists countered by saying that the real world involved issues affecting everyone: economic justice, civil rights, clean environment, etc.

Enmeshed in their own point of view, neither side was able to see the obvious truth: that the distinction between the spiritual realm and the material realm is an artificial one we have devised for our own purposes. We had to do something to counter the Incarnation! As readers of this journal know only too well, that "Word Become Flesh" action by the Adversary remains the single most devastating blow to our Cause.

Earlier in this essay I mentioned "two primary movements" in the Grovedale parish that called for my attention. I have detailed how I successfully dealt with the first of these, the spiritual growth threat. The second is more difficult to describe.

To begin with, this second factor at Grovedale was not a threat so much as an opportunity. To call it a "movement" is probably misleading. It would be more accurate to describe it as a theological position, though that implies the humans in this camp are theologically articulate. Most of them are not. But nearly all of them, whether they are political activists or totally uninterested in social issues, share the conviction that no real opposition exists between the Christian faith and life in the world with its demands and compromises. Another way of saying it is that they refuse to acknowledge the reality of evil. This denial is rooted in a deep-seated fear of death, a fear which it is in our best interests to promote while at the same time keeping under wraps.

While they may call themselves Christians, the object of their worship is not really the Adversary. Instead, many of them worship an idea — the idea of success, of *improvement*. This worship takes many forms. In the life of the church, it may focus on beautifying the building, strengthening the music program, increasing the budget. In the social realm, it results in campaigns for better health care, less unemployment, an end to apartheid. On a personal level, it supports a push for an increased standard of living, a more prestigious job, a chance to send the kids to a name university.

All of these goals are universally accepted as being worthwhile, even noble. Many Grovedale members include petitions for them in their prayers. But such prayers are mostly a matter of form. What they really believe is that they can attain these goals by their own efforts. The Adversary is regarded, at best, as a psychological boost for their endeavors.

You can see how the rise of the spiritual growth movement in the congregation would make many Grovedale members uncomfortable. I encouraged the critics of the spiritual growth people to use words like "naive" and "unsophisticated" to describe their peers who were engaging in Bible study and prayer. I assured the critics that they were perfectly justified in believing that they could improve their own lives and the lives of humanity by pursuing worthwhile goals without the added "baggage" of spiritual discipline.

This tactic works wonderfully! We want humans to *accustom* themselves to the world they live in, to ignore the fact that the life of the Christian in the world is necessarily "scandalous." We must keep them from being consciously aware that our Malevolent Lord is the ruler of the world. It is really a wonder we can still get away with it, considering the evidence of evil in this era the earthlings call the twentieth century. How any earthling, especially Christians, can deny the power of Death all around them is beyond me. You would think they had never heard of the Cross! One has to feel a bit sorry for them, really. They suppose that by living decent lives, by trying very hard to do good, they can make everything come out right, whether it be a troubled marriage or an international crisis. This pathetic illusion keeps them safely distanced from the Adversary's camp.

Most of them think of "sin" as a hopelessly outmoded idea and "the devil" as a myth from the Dark

Ages. Our best strategy is to keep them thinking just
this way. Failing that, we must get them to confine
their definition of "sin" to one of *individual* foibles.
Our problems begin when humans understand the cor-
porate nature of sin, how the folly of any one of their
family, community, or nation implicates all. When they
reach this stage, it is much harder to get them to
delude themselves with optimism about human intel-
lect, strength, and goodness. They are then ripe to
apprehend the truth of that biblical phrase so wonderfully true and yet so dangerous for us when humans
contemplate it: "There is none righteous, no not one."
Once the implications of that truth sink in, we may
have lost everything.

Fortunately, there is little danger of that circumstance at Grovedale right now. I have scored a
triumph by employing a perennially successful tactic:
the temptation to hubris. I have used the trappings of a
large and superficially successful church program to
lead them into thinking they can accomplish great
things. In reality, the most they can "accomplish" is to
perpetuate their successful image of themselves. In
other words, I have managed to make them content
with the "means." If you ask members of Grovedale to
describe their church, they can tell you a great deal
about the building, the music program, the educational
program, and the budget. But, if you ask them what
the point of all this effort is, they will give you a blank
stare.

In summary, I believe my accomplishments at
Grovedale can serve as a model for agents of the Prince
of Darkness in nearly any church on Earth. My specific
methods need not be duplicated, but the essential
strategy has universal application: 1) assess the situation; 2) zero in on the strengths of a church; and 3) use
the dark side of those strengths to subvert and corrupt.

10.

Last Record

Groacher's reassignment to Grovedale is his last field assignment documented in the files to which I had access. After an unbroken series of fiascoes, it is ironic that Groacher's career should reach the kind of success detailed in the preceding chapter and then all record of his activity suddenly come to an end.

However, there is an explanation for the abrupt ending to the record of information about Groacher's doings. Apparently climbing the ladder in Hell is fraught with as many dangers as on earth. So long as Groacher had the reputation of a bumbler, he enjoyed the kind of camaraderie that universally exists among those of the same rank. But when his work at Grovedale won him a measure of fame, the situation changed. Not surprisingly, envy has a prominent place in Hell. That Groacher became a victim of it is also not surprising, as the final document in the Groacher file makes clear. Unlike many of the letters, reports, and other materials in the file, this one is a fragment. Neither the sender of what appears to be a memo nor its recipient is indicated. Nevertheless, internal evidence makes it clear that the memo was sent during the second Grovedale period to Groacher's immediate superior, one Babisch Gobghast. It becomes obvious that Gobghast indulged Groacher by giving him more opportunity to conduct his own program than demonic supervisors are wont to do. The sender of this final memo criticizes this approach and then takes up the crux of the matter: an administrative decision with dire implications for Groacher.

The identity of the demon who wrote the following communication remains a mystery.

. . .Nonetheless, Gobghast, your handling of the Groacher situation can be faulted in several respects. Most telling was your leniency in matters of procedure. Granted, we do allow supervisors, especially those like yourself with commendable track records, some leeway in dealing with agents under their jurisdiction. But you very nearly gave Groacher a free hand in the Grovedale assignment. That comes dangerously close to dereliction of duty on your part.

The shortsightedness of you middle management types has become almost epidemic lately. Many of you resist what you disdainfully call "going by the book." Such arrogance blinds you to the long term results of allowing field agents to chart their own course. May I remind you that the title "supervisor" implies supervision! In one of your reports you have the temerity to refer, with implied approval, to "Agent Groacher's flair for creative improvisation."

Idiot! The heresy of your language alone is grounds for censure. The gratuitous use of all derivatives of the word "create" is forbidden in official communications, as you surely must know. Why the Adversary stupidly chose to share the divine prerogative of creation with the earthlings is totally incomprehensible to us. It is also none of our concern. That this capability is denied to us is maddening, of course. Some demons choose to deal with their frustration in this regard by resorting to cynicism about the creative process and about what humans choose to call art. Such an attitude is counterproductive. A far more commendable approach is to twist the creative impulse in humans so that the actual results are far different from what the Adversary intended.

With the proper touch, we can take the artistic gifts of a writer, let us say, and distort them enough to produce books that are all but devoid of goodness. We have become expert in seducing humans, on whom the Adversary has bestowed varied talents, into using such gifts for their own ego trips, rather than for glorifying the Source of these gifts. Even more wonderfully fiendish is the way we have persuaded so many earthlings that creativity is the province and privilege of only a handful of artists or musicians or poets, that "an average person like me" has nothing creative to offer. No, we demons cannot create. But we can destroy or, failing that, we can at least corrupt the creative impulse.

In any case, your flippant use of the word "create" cannot be countenanced. A similar transgression in the future will be met with appropriate measures. In the meantime, you will submit to me as part of your next report a synopsis of the "Usage and Vocabulary" chapter in *The Manual of Style for Hadesian Writers*.

It is obvious to me that your *laissez faire* approach to Groacher was the chief cause of his misconduct. The reports of his success with the Grovedale situation aroused our interest at once. How could a demon who had made such a mess of things everywhere else suddenly achieve such an amazing turnaround? Our investigation revealed that Groacher's methods, while somewhat unorthodox, were generally sound. It looked as though his previous experiences had taught him what was really needed in the task of subversion and corruption.

What a teeth-gnashing frustration when we discovered his malfeasance! We learned of it with no thanks to you. (You can indeed be grateful that our investigation found your failure to report it was due to ignorance on your part rather than collaboration.) Without the tip we received from an agent jealous of

Groacher's success (his identity is classified information), it would have taken us Satan-knows-how long to
spot what was happening to Groacher.

Luckily, we identified the problem in time. But I
must warn you that any subsequent failure to report the
Adversary's encroachment into your territory will have
the gravest of consequences. You must constantly be on
the alert, especially at the points where your agents
have been achieving successes. I hasten to add what I
am sure you already know: that this acknowledgment
of the Adversary's power extending into our realm must
remain strictly off the record. As senior executives, we
must of necessity deal with the reality of Heaven's vile
arm stretching this far. All others in Hell must be kept
in ignorance of it. After Groacher's rehabilitation, all
memory of Heaven's contact with him will vanish from
his mind.

Let me return to the matter at hand. One of the
first clues that Groacher had come under the influence
of the Other Side was his ability to laugh at himself. In
one of his reports to you, he refers to his newly found
"sense of the ridiculous." That should have been a tip-
off. Reference to personal pleasure of any kind is cause
for alarm, and even an oblique reference to humor or
laughter should have sent up red flags in your mind.
And how could you have overlooked Groacher's alarming comment in another report: "I find the saving
grace of laughter in these humans to be one of their
most endearing traits'?

Far more serious, of course, was the sympathy
Groacher began to demonstrate for the people of
Grovedale. It was not readily apparent at first. He
seemed to hold them in the same disdain as previously,
an attitude we stress in our training program. But
slowly there crept into Groacher's language evidence of
a grudging respect for the humans' courage and resil-

ence in the face of their own frailty and, as Groacher himself put it, "the heartache and the thousand natural shocks that flesh is heir to."* That was another clue, by the way. When a demon begins quoting Shakespeare with approbation, he or she must be watched closely. Earthling art, even of the pagan variety and even that which we have managed to subvert, imbibes enough of the Adversary's own being to be extremely dangerous.

But it was in his celebrated article that appeared in *Harpies' Monthly* that Groacher gave the whole thing away. I refer to his bald statement that "one has to feel a bit sorry for them." I should not have to point out to you, Gobghast, that such a sentiment is treasonable. That it got into print at all is the fault of the editor; you can be sure he has been called to account for his criminal negligence. Your failure to insist that Groacher delete this statement from his article is yet another blot on your record.

The final nail in the coffin of Groacher's career, however, came in his last memo to you. Our requirement that copies of all communications between supervisors and their subordinates be transmitted to headquarters for review is intended for just such situations. When you failed to report Groacher's blasphemous and traitorous statement, we moved in quickly. I refer, of course, to the ending of Groacher's last memo which I quote, to refresh your memory:

> Sometimes watching the activities and reading over the shoulders of the Grovedale Christians can have strange effects on me. Most of what they write and read consists of the most pitiful trash imaginable. But recently I received a jolt. In one of the prayer groups, someone read the words of Martin

ED. NOTE: actually, a quote from Shakespeare's Hamlet.

Niemoller who was recounting the spiritual lessons he had learned during his eight-year imprisonment under Hitler. ''God is not the enemy of my enemies,'' wrote Niemoller. ''God is not even the enemy of God's own enemies.''

For a terrifying moment, I found myself wanting, more than anything I've ever wanted, to believe this was true. Oh, I know such a belief flies in the face of everything I've been taught; we do not admit the possibility that the Adversary can be anything but the Adversary to us demons. But what if it *were* possible? What if . . .?''

When confronted with the evidence against him, Groacher, to his credit, did not deny that he had written the statement. He accepted his consignment to the Waters of Lethe Reprogramming Center with commendable stoicism.

I need only add that your supervision of Groacher's replacement will be watched with great interest by headquarters. One slip on your part and . . .

Ken Gibble

Don't let Ken Gibble's beard throw you: he is really a die-hard Phillies' fan disguised as a minister! As an ex-softball player, Ken now takes great delight in his 12-year old daughter's softball and basketball skills. As a minister, he participates in a unique co-pastorate with his wife Ann at the Arlington Church of the Brethren (Arlington, Virginia).

A former teacher of English, with a Master of Divinity and a Doctor of Ministry from Bethany Theological Seminary (Oakbrook, Illinois), Ken now extends his many skill areas into teaching at Wesley Theological Seminary (Washington, D.C.), doing free-lance writing for numerous magazines and journals, and working as a promotion consultant for the MESSENGER (a Church of the Brethren magazine).

Ken describes himself as a "preacher/storyteller": "after all, preaching is really telling The Story." He is an avid reader, a movie-goer whenever he gets the chance, and a lover of drama. He has several published plays and thoroughly enjoys directing, acting, and scriptwriting. He is also the author of five published books. But Ken is not one to do all of his writing behind a desk! He often takes an assignment to write a travel article so he has an excuse to go out biking, take pictures, and walk outdoors.